From Rock and Tempest

FROM ROCK AND TEMPEST

The Life of
Captain George William Manby

by

KENNETH WALTHEW

GEOFFREY BLES · LONDON

© KENNETH WALTHEW, 1971

SBN: 7138 0287 1

Printed in Great Britain
by Richard Clay (The Chaucer Press), Ltd.,
Bungay, Suffolk

Published by
GEOFFREY BLES LTD
52 Doughty Street, London, W.C.1.N 2.L.Z
36–38 Clarence Street, Sydney, N.S.W. 2000
353 Elizabeth Street, Melbourne, C.1
246 Queen Street, Brisbane
CML Building, King William Street, Adelaide, S.A. 5000
P.O. Box 37, Claremont, W.A. 6010
Lake Road, Northcote, Auckland
100 Lesmill Road, Don Mills, Ontario
P.O. Box 8879, Johannesburg
P.O. Box 834, Cape Town
P.O. Box 2800, Salisbury, Rhodesia

'From rock and tempest, fire and foe,
Protect them wheresoe'er they go . . .'

WILLIAM WHITING
Hymn '*For those in peril on the sea*'

ILLUSTRATIONS

7

Illustrations

Illustrations are reproduced by courtesy of the following:

[1] British Museum
[2] National Maritime Museum
[3] Royal National Lifeboat Institution
[4] King's Lynn Museum
[5] Schermuly Limited
[6] Central Library, Great Yarmouth

ACKNOWLEDGMENTS

IN THE COURSE of writing this book, I am aware that I made myself a great nuisance to a large number of people. Without exception, my importunities were endured with remarkable patience and good humour. For this, and for the help and encouragement I received, I am most grateful.

My thanks are due, in particular, to the Librarian of the Wren Library, Trinity College, Cambridge, who guided me through the labyrinth of the Dawson Turner Correspondence; to Miss A. S. Mottram, Curator at King's Lynn, Mr A. C. Hedges, Librarian at Great Yarmouth, and Mr C. R. Elliott of the Royal National Lifeboat Institution, for their invaluable help in my research; to Messrs. Schermuly, Ltd, who lent me much interesting material from their archives, and to the Editor of *The Coastguard* for his assistance and advice.

I am also indebted to the staff of the British Museum, the National Maritime Museum and the Public Records Office, who gave me the benefit of their expert knowledge.

K.W.

I

AT THE MOST easterly point of England, mid-way between the Thames estuary and the Wash, is the Norfolk town of Great Yarmouth. Sandwiched by the North Sea and a marshy hinterland where bleak winds blow against the broken sails of decaying windmills, Great Yarmouth, surprisingly, is a popular holiday resort. It is a brash, thriving town, geared to the supermarket world of today, and visitors are not encouraged to waste their spending time delving into its history. Vestiges of the past, which have survived German bombs and demolition gangs, seem to be there on sufferance, to be removed as soon as possible.

On the seafront, in this state of suspended sentence, are two obstinate relics of the nineteenth century. They are both stone monuments, and one, the smaller of the two, commemorates Captain George William Manby and his invention for throwing a line to stranded ships by means of a gun. Manby's monument is a three-foot cube of granite, on top of which a spherical ornament supports a grappling-iron. It stands on the pavement, and holiday-makers find it obstructs their lawful passage between the electronic bingo and the candyfloss booth. Opposite, across the wide, bustling promenade, is the fun-fair. The Big Wheel turns against the sky, and as the Giant Dipper plunges, shrieks of delighted terror rise above the incessant blare of pop music. Beyond the fun-fair is the sandy beach which is the basis of Yarmouth's prosperity, and beyond that, the sharp North Sea. Over all, the fumes of fish and chips hang like a greasy pall.[1] They penetrate everywhere, permeate everything.

The second monument is a quarter of a mile away where the promenade ends and the docks begin at the mouth of the river Yare. The Navy has long ago deserted Yarmouth, and so, to a great extent, has the fishing fleet; but there are always ships berthed along the quays, unloading timber from Scandinavia, or taking on cargoes of rusty scrap-iron for unimaginable destinations. The monument, surrounded by factories and dwarfed by a vast new power station, is set a little way back from the road. It is more elaborate than Manby's—a circular column some two hundred feet high, surmounted by the figure of Britannia, gilded once, but now tarnished to the same dirty grey as the stone. This monument celebrates Admiral Lord Nelson, and around the plinth are carved the names of his victories.

When it was built, Nelson's monument was the pride of Yarmouth. It stood alone in the middle of a broad expanse of grassland, unobstructed to the sea. The acres have shrunk, and now there is only a patch of sour, uncared for turf, strewn with litter. There are steps leading to an entrance in the base, and there is a notice saying that persons entering the monument do so at their own risk. What is inside, and what the hazards are, remain mysterious, for the door is locked, and the threshold piled with years of accumulated rubbish.

There is a link between these two neglected stone memorials on the front at Great Yarmouth. Manby and Nelson were contemporaries; they were both Norfolk men; they went to school together at Downham. Manby was very proud of his friendship with Nelson; but mixed with this pride was a sense of injustice. He knew that he was equally deserving of the nation's gratitude. He was filled with a desperate longing for fame and honour, but for him, however frantically he strove after them, they were always part of a wonderful tomorrow.

The Nelson column was built and paid for by the citizens of Yarmouth after Nelson's death. Manby could not trust posterity; he designed and erected his own stone while he was still living. There was only one place he could put it, and that was the tiny front garden of his villa in the suburb of Southtown. Later tenants found it an inconvenience; the Corporation reluctantly took it over and gave it its present resting place on the front.

Because of Manby and his inventions, thousands have been saved from a terrible death by shipwreck and fire. Fortunes have been made from the exploitation of some of Manby's ideas; but other men have taken both the credit and the profit. Manby lived in debt and died in debt, so that even the stone he put up to himself was mortgaged.

Manby was a simple man; quadratic equations were quite beyond him, and he read only one book—*Robinson Crusoe*—in his life. The ideas that flowed from his brain were also simple—anyone could have thought of them—just, as Manby once pointed out, anyone could have discovered America 'if the thought had struck them'. An extraordinary variety of thoughts struck Manby, ranging from naval gunnery to the establishment of a convict colony in Greenland, but there was a dominant theme, an obsession that finally ruined him, and this was the saving of human life.

Manby assumed that humanity would be grateful, and would reward him in a fitting manner. Long and bitter experience proved him to be wrong. He met obstruction and prejudice where he might have expected the greatest encouragement—from the very people he was trying to save. Three kings and a queen treated him with an indifference verging on contempt. Successive governments regarded him as a crank and a nuisance, and the help they gave was tardy and parsimonious. It never occurred to Manby that he himself might be partly at fault. The rightness of his own behaviour was something he never questioned; but, in fact, not all his peculiarities were endearing, and some of them could only be excused on grounds of insanity. It could also be argued that he overestimated the value of himself and his work, and that his exaggerated, tediously repeated claims only served to make him ridiculous.

No doubt he was, in many ways, ridiculous. A vein of comedy was embedded in his nature. It showed through at even the most solemn moments—when someone tried to murder him, for instance, or when he met Princess Victoria.

The comedy was classic, never far from pathos, and it was rooted in Manby's own total inability to see the joke. But taken over all, his life was a tragedy, and it was mankind's tragedy as much as Manby's.

In the year 1803, Yarmouth, besides being a port and a naval depot of some importance, was a pleasant, spacious little town, growing in popularity as a health resort. In its dowdy, East Anglian way, it was quite gay. There were the Assembly Rooms for concerts, balls and amateur theatricals; there were fêtes, military bands and a ritual Sunday morning fashion parade on the wide meadows between the sea and the river; and, adding spice and interest to life, there were the sailors from the elegant warships anchored in the Roads.

Yarmouth, like any seaport, particularly in time of war, had its seamier side. It attracted many dubious characters, prepared to cater, at a price, to a startling variety of inclinations, and among the more respectable of these was a fortune-teller called Mrs Williams. Mrs Williams, threatened with arrest and imprisonment in London, had gravitated to Yarmouth. She was reputed to possess remarkable powers and soon established a profitable business. One of her most convinced devotees was Mrs Sleogin, the youngish widow of a naval officer. Inevitably, Mrs Williams foresaw that her client would soon remarry; naturally, Mrs Sleogin was anxious to identify her next husband and, since it seemed likely that he would be among them, she took a lively interest in the unattached gentlemen of Yarmouth.

In particular, she took an interest in Captain Manby who lodged in the same modest boarding-house as herself. The Captain, although he claimed to have shipped in men-of-war, was not a sailor. He was in the Army, and had recently been appointed Master of Yarmouth barracks. For a military man, he was unusually small, but his slight physique was more than compensated by an aggressive vitality and an apparently inexhaustible nervous energy. He dressed with fastidious elegance, was a great organiser of social events and clearly regarded himself as the Beau Brummell of Yarmouth. He did not seem to have any fortune—in fact, he was said to be heavily in debt—but he was, unquestionably, a gentleman.

As far as Mrs Sleogin could discover, Captain Manby had no wife or family; but the rumours, passed with the teacups, suggested a chequered, romantic and even a violent past. There were hints of a duel, and of gunshot wounds in the head.

Captain Manby talked a great deal, principally about himself; but his accounts were confined to the more reputable aspects of his history. He came, she gathered, from an ancient Yorkshire family, and was extremely proud that he could trace his ancestry back to the reign of Henry the Second. His paternal grandfather had been an officer in the Customs, at a time when a shrewd man could benefit himself as well as the Revenue. With the fortune he accumulated, he bought Denver Hall, an estate on the fringe of the fens, and established himself as a country squire. Manby had been born at Denver Hall, and he was fond of describing its ornamental chimneys, tall turrets and gabled roof—all curiously ornate in the bleak setting of flat, black silt, drainage dykes and Roman roads.

When Manby spoke of his parents, it was with nostalgic affection. His mother had been both beautiful and virtuous, while his father, he said, had combined the qualities of a gallant soldier with those of a kind and indulgent parent. Matthew Pepper Manby had fought with Wolfe at Quebec, and later served as aide-de-camp to Lord Townshend when Lord Lieutenant of Ireland. Manby was careful to include in his anecdotes the fact that at his christening in Denver church, Lord Townshend had been his godfather.

Soon after this christening, the family moved to a larger estate, Wood Hall, a few miles away at Hilgay on the banks of the river Wissey. Here, in a gracious Tudor mansion of rosy brick, the Manbys multiplied. A new addition was an almost annual event; but of the seven children who were born at Wood Hall, only three—his brother Thomas and two sisters—survived beyond the age of ten.

When he was five, Manby became a day boy at a small school in the nearby town of Downham Market. This was an event which was to acquire an enormous significance, for at the same school was a boy called Horatio Nelson, the son of a country parson. Nelson was seven years older than Manby, and shortly, at the age of twelve, to enter the Navy. Since the school was divided into two separate houses, senior and junior, it is doubtful if Manby could have been more than vaguely aware of Nelson's presence, and even more improbable that Nelson knew of Manby's existence. Yet from the way Manby talked, it appeared they had been close and intimate friends.

Mrs Sleogin learnt a great deal about Nelson, for Manby recalled, or imagined he could recall, every detail, down to the colour—pea-green—of the little jacket Nelson had worn as a boy. More remarkable still, he could remember conversations, the games they had played together and how Nelson had demonstrated precocious nautical talent in mock battles with paper boats,

Captain G. W. Manby

CAPTAIN MANBY'S MORTAR LIFE-LINE.

Woodcut from the *Illustrated London News*, 1843

launched on the stream beside the pump on the market square at Downham. He went even further, and claimed that Horatio had been a regular visitor to Wood Hall, returning with Manby in the dog-cart on Saturday afternoons and staying until the following Monday.[2]

Nelson's fame and glory were a powerful stimulant to Manby's memory. He had come, it seemed, to identify himself with the hero. On the flimsy basis of what, at the most, was a very short and remote childhood acquaintance, he had concocted a mythology—almost a religion—in which he featured not only as a part of Nelson but also, in a peculiar way, as responsible for him.

Despite the boy's uncertain health and diminutive size, his father decided that Manby should follow him into the Army, and when he was twelve he was packed off to the Tower of London where there was a preparatory school for budding artillery officers. The emphasis here was on mathematics; unfortunately Manby found he had 'an unconquerable dislike of the subject from its abstruseness'. Although he contrived to crib his way into the Royal Military Academy at Woolwich, the Faculty decided, after four years of struggle, that he would never make a gunner, and his military ambitions were reduced to part-time soldiering in the Cambridge Militia.

At this point, Manby's recollections of his youth became vague and unsatisfactory. The only solid fact Mrs Sleogin could glean was that, at the death of his father, he had inherited Wood Hall and become the Lord of the Manor of Hilgay. This, however impressive, left a large question mark looming over the things Mrs Sleogin most wanted to know. What was the Lord of the Manor of Hilgay doing as Barrack Master of Yarmouth? Why was Lord Townshend's godson and Nelson's dearest friend living in a cheap boarding-house, avoiding his tailor? And most crucial of all, what, if she had ever existed, had happened to the Lady of the Manor? Captain Manby was a mystery, and a very aggravating one to Mrs Sleogin, who decided to seek the help of Mrs Williams.

With determined guile, she wheedled from the Captain the time and date of his birth—six o'clock on the evening of November 28th, 1765. She confided this information to Mrs Williams, who, having studied her astral charts, produced an intriguing horoscope.

'The person,' she told Mrs Sleogin, 'whose past, present and future you take so deep an interest in, has suffered mental affliction almost unparalleled, and I greatly fear that she who vowed at the altar to love and cherish him, has not only been the cause of it, but instigated an attempt on his assassination. He will undertake pursuits that will obtain for him the highest credit and load him with honours; he will live to a good old age and die the happiest of men.'

Manby had always professed a sturdy disbelief in fortune-telling; but when Mrs Sleogin coyly related what Mrs Williams had seen in the stars, he changed his mind. It was astounding; the past had already happened, and as for the future, he knew instinctively—had always known—that great achievements and high honours awaited him. In that moment his scepticism changed to a lifelong belief in clairvoyance. He was that sort of man; once he had decided to believe, no argument, no evidence, no subsequent event, could move him.

Manby did have gunshot wounds in the head. He had acquired them, in circumstances that are rather confused, when he was shot at by his first wife's lover, a Captain Pogson of the East India Company. To explain why the damage was to the back of his head, Manby claimed that Pogson had crept up behind him on a beach in South Wales, and had shot him while he was getting into a boat.[3] The opposing story was that Manby had been running away from a duel, but whatever the manner of the shooting, when it occurred, Manby was known to have been wearing a hat. This seemingly trivial detail was, in fact, of the utmost importance. The shot, passing through the hat, forced bits of felt into his skull.

In time the felt rotted and became poisonous. Sixteen months after the shooting, he endured a series of crude operations—the most painful, he said, mortal ever underwent—to remove the slugs and the embedded fragments of putrid material. In the process his brain was exposed and damaged in a way that had peculiar effects on his personality. He survived to live to the age of eighty-nine, but he was never completely sane after the surgeon had finished probing his skull.

Manby kept the lead shot that had been taken out of his head, and carried it about with him in a little ivory box. As for the head itself, he left this, as a deferred payment of fees, to his doctor. 'I shall lay as quiet in my grave without it,' he said. He hoped it would eventually be deposited in the first anatomical museum in the country. Great public good, he thought, would result.[4]

Barrack Master, although not wholly a sinecure, was, nevertheless, a very comfortable and sought-after appointment, and particularly was this so of Yarmouth Barracks. There were no troops permanently stationed at Yarmouth; the barracks were maintained for militia training and to accommodate regiments on the march. Provided there was an efficient Barrack Sergeant, the duties of Master were nominal, and consisted mainly of entertaining visiting officers. In the manner of most desirable government posts at this time, Barrack Master usually came to a man through influence or nepotism. Manby got the job in a way that was probably unique; he put his foot in the front door of the Secretary at War, and refused, despite threats of violence, to move it.

It was not Manby's intention when he wedged open Charles Yorke's[5] front door, to solicit an appointment as Barrack Master. He had come to offer his services to assassinate Napoleon. Manby, the professional murderer, on the steps of the great London house, was shabby, haggard and wild-eyed. It was hardly surprising that the porter told him curtly that Mr Yorke was not at home, and attempted to slam the door in his face. Manby, his foot firmly positioned, said, according to his own account: 'You may make me a cripple, but you shall not defeat the object of my enquiry. I come on a special service to make a personal and immediate communication to your master.'

The porter's response was to shout for help, and a number of bulky footmen appeared. Throwing an importunate caller down the area steps was not, in those days, an uncommon duty for the servants of the rich and powerful. Normally the incident would have passed without remark, and without disturbing the master of the house. But Manby put up a struggle, and created an uproar out of all proportion to his size. The noise brought Yorke himself into the hall.

The Minister was astonished when he recognised the frantic little man on the point of being summarily ejected. Manby had been a fellow officer in the Cambridge Militia, and Yorke had reason to remember him with gratitude. It was Manby who had stepped in as peacemaker when, after an exchange of intoxicated insults in the mess, Yorke had found himself challenged to a duel. It was Manby too, who, single-handed, had quelled an incipient mutiny when the regiment had been on manoeuvres in Essex. If it had not been for Manby they might all have been murdered in their tents. Feet unequal to the strain of Army life had obliged Manby to resign his commission.[6] Since that time, as far as Yorke knew, he had inherited a substantial property in Norfolk; had married and settled down as a gentleman farmer. How to account, then, for this disreputable figure fighting footmen on the doorstep?

When Manby had been released, dusted down and given a glass of wine, the explanation came pouring out. It was true he had inherited Wood Hall from his father; it was true he had married; but it was not true he had settled down. His life, in fact, since he had hobbled away from the regiment in the spring of 1793, had been a series of disasters. In an incredibly short space of time he had lost his money, his land, his mansion and his wife. He had very nearly lost his life, and was now certainly on the verge of losing his reason.

The girl he had married, shortly after his twenty-eighth birthday, was Jane Preston, the daughter of a Suffolk rector who had been a close friend of his father. Jane, an only child, was beautiful; but she was also spoilt, capricious and idiotically extravagant. Manby, for a Norfolk man, was unusually incompetent in matters of money and business. Together they formed a combination which might have been designed for bankruptcy.

It had taken Manby and his wife five years to run through their fortune. The final crash was accelerated by foolish speculation, and a flood which ruined crops and drowned livestock. Creditors became pressing; mortgagers foreclosed. They sold Wood Hall and fled to South Wales, where Manby tried to scrape a living writing guide books, and Jane, already tired of poverty and a husband who seemed to fail at everything he tried, found consolation in the arms of Captain Pogson.

After Pogson had shot Manby in the back of the head, he left the country hurriedly, taking Jane with him. The shooting, among its many repercussions, seriously disturbed Manby's creditors. A target was not a sound risk; demands for immediate settlement became more urgent and less polite, and when they were not met, Manby was arrested for debt.

He was rescued from prison by his brother Thomas, now a Captain in the Navy, a handsome, dashing young man who had just returned from voyaging round the world with Vancouver. Later in life he was to have notoriety thrust upon him as one of a number of dashing young naval officers accused by her husband, the Prince of Wales, of scandalous behaviour with Princess Caroline.[7] It was even to be suggested, but never proved, that he was the father of her illegitimate son.[8] At the time he bailed his brother out of the debtors' prison, Thomas seemed to be on the threshold of a brilliant career, and had just been given command of the frigate *Bordelais*, a smart, fast little ship which had been captured from the French.

Manby's affairs were in such a hopeless state that it was clear that, if he stayed in Wales, he would soon be back in prison. His brother suggested he joined the crew of the *Bordelais* and, since there seemed no other suitable job for him, he was appointed lay chaplain. Manby had visions of restoring his fortune and his reputation by heroic behaviour in battles with the French Revolutionaries; the voyage, however, on which they embarked early in April 1800, was merely to Dublin. This should have been routine and uneventful; but nothing, it seemed, in which Manby was concerned ever turned out quite as expected.

The *Bordelais*, although elegant in appearance, was unstable in the water and difficult to handle. They ran into foul weather off the Irish coast, and foundered on the Arklow Bank. This incident made a deep impression upon Manby. It brought home to him dramatically the paradox that ships were in their greatest peril, not on the high seas, but when they were in shallow waters and in sight of land. A sailing vessel, however skilfully handled, was always, to a large extent, at the mercy of the elements. Well away from land, there was a reasonable chance of weathering the fiercest storm, but once blown on to a lee shore the prospects of survival were slight. It was usually impossible to reach the beach either by swimming or launching a boat, because of waves, rocks and the deadly whirlpool of the surf. For the same reasons, assistance could rarely be expected from the land. The crew of a grounded vessel were trapped in a fragile wooden structure which would almost inevitably be smashed to fragments.

'The striking of the ship,' Manby recorded, 'was the most awful and momentous period I had hitherto experienced. The immediate hallooing of all hands on deck; to the pumps, plumb the well, cut away the masts, throw the guns overboard. And amid all this activity, the dismal moans of some, the screams of the women.'

The prompt action in throwing everything portable overboard saved the *Bordelais*. A huge wave carried her off the bank, leaving fifty-eight feet of keel behind. By the time they had limped back to Plymouth, and the damage had been repaired, it was the end of May. They were given orders to cruise the Atlantic in search of three large French ships, believed to be lurking to intercept the homeward bound Brazil fleet.

Meanwhile, the bits of hat in Manby's skull had rotted, the operations to remove the slugs had taken place and he lay, desperately ill, in cheap lodgings in Plymouth.

'Considering death inevitable,' he wrote later, 'I preferred to die at sea among sailors (a consoling and compassionate class of man) rather than be left in the care of a mistress of lodgings, to be hurried to my grave unnoticed and unknown.'

A party of sailors from the *Bordelais* arrived early one morning, wrapped their lay chaplain in blankets and carried him through the streets on board the ship. Once at sea, instead of dying, Manby underwent a remarkable recovery. For eight weeks they cruised the sunny Azores, returning to Plymouth without having fired a shot or seen a Frenchman. It had been a pleasant holiday, an experience Manby was to look back upon with nostalgia for the rest of his life. It was also the end of his naval career. There was news awaiting at Plymouth that his sister Maria had died at King's Lynn. He left the *Bordelais* and hurried across the country to the east coast. While he was away, his ship came under orders, and sailed without him, bound for the West Indies.

With a small legacy from his sister, Manby foolishly decided to go back to South Wales. If he expected that everything would now be forgotten and forgiven, he was wrong. His creditors were waiting, and this time they were determined he should not escape. In a few months his legacy had disappeared. He fended off starvation and prison by selling, one by one, the few pieces of family silver that had survived the crash.

At this time, Napoleon was rampaging through Europe. It

seemed likely that he would very soon be rampaging through England as well. The Duke of York, Commander-in-Chief, in the time he could spare from his complicated love life, had devised various schemes to meet the contingency. A string of Martello towers were hastily being built around the coast, and there was an extraordinary plan to inundate the approaches to the capital. In Manby's opinion, these measures were futile. To his mind, there was only one certain way of preventing Napoleon invading England, and that was to kill him before he set out. Manby put forward this thesis in a pamphlet,[9] followed by an offer to the government to undertake the murder personally. The letter passed slowly across the desks of Whitehall. Eventually Manby received his answer: the plan, although not without merit, was considered unstatesmanlike.

When Manby had reached his last piece of silver, and was faced with utter destitution, he decided on one final, desperate bid to recover his fortune and bring fame and honour upon himself. He spent his last few shillings to travel to London, intent on persuading his old friend, now Secretary at War, to allow him to go to France and assassinate Napoleon.

Yorke listened sympathetically to Manby's bizarre story. When it had finished, he remarked: 'Manby, you are deserving of a better fate.' He did not give the little man leave to murder Napoleon; but when Manby left the house, he was Master of Yarmouth Barracks, and held the rank of Lieutenant-Captain.

2

FOR A FEW YEARS life was very pleasant for the new Barrack
Master of Yarmouth. Now that he had status and a regular pay
cheque, he could look his creditors in the face, even though he
might not pay them, while the local tradesmen were quite happy
to let him run up new accounts. He soon moved from the
boarding-house, and took up residence at the barracks. The desperate man who a few months earlier had set out to murder
Napoleon, was transformed into a gaily coloured social butterfly,
flitting between town and barracks, entertaining and being enter-
tained.

In his own opinion, he was exceptionally well qualified as a
leader in matters of manners and fashion. In his twenties, after he
had been rejected as an artillery officer, he had lived as a man-
about-town in London. On the bohemian fringes of high society,
he had rubbed shoulders with the rich and dissolute, the celebrated
and notorious. There was a discreet house in Charles Street, where,

for an entrance fee of half-a-guinea, ladies and gentlemen could meet in an unconventional way. He was small, lively, quaint; a bouncing, miniature dandy. Women found him attractive, and among his conquests was the sexually ambiguous Chevalier d'Eon, at this time playing a female role.[1] Who in Yarmouth could match sophistication of this calibre?

The country was at war, on the verge of bankruptcy and liable to be invaded at any moment; but all this did not deter the Navy from enjoying life. While their ships lay in the Roads, nominally in a state of readiness, the captains led frequent rollicking forays ashore. They were rowed in state into the harbour; hired carriages awaited them on the quay, with pretty ladies inside and picnic hampers on the boot. 'Amid great mirth and hilarity,' Manby recorded tactfully, 'they set off for a cruise into the country, for the enjoyment of shooting, et cetera.'[2]

When they could not come ashore, they threw lavish parties on their ships. Manby was frequently invited. He was accepted, as other miserable lieutenant-captains in the Army would not have been, partly because of his brother, and partly because of his willingness to make himself useful. He devised a kite to carry mail to the flagship when gales interrupted communication with the shore, and he kept watch for enemy ships while the Navy was away on its sporting expeditions. He seemed, at that time, a harmless and amusing little man.

They were pleasant years, but for a man of forty who had a great destiny to fulfil, they seemed to be leading nowhere. The achievements which Mrs Williams had foreseen were still undefined. Apart from his mail-carrying kite, he had shown no evidence of inventive talent. He had shown, in fact, little evidence of any talent whatever, except as an artist. Drawing was one subject in which he had excelled at the Military Academy, and he had taught himself engraving to illustrate his guide books.[3] But even his drawing was at an amateur level, and art, he knew, would never be the ultimate source of his fame. The fanaticism which marked the later stages of his career was dormant; it was difficult to be a fanatic without a cause.

Although these first years as Barrack Master seemed outwardly to be unproductive, one circumstance gave them a peculiar importance. He became the close friend of a man called Dawson Turner,[4] and this was to have a decisive bearing on his whole future. There could hardly have been a more unlikely friendship, for Dawson Turner was, in almost every way, the complete opposite of Manby. A banker by profession, he was also a distinguished naturalist and a patron of the arts. He was rich, respectable and cultured; a model of commercial integrity and domestic virtue. The two men first met through Turner's wife who, like Manby, was an accomplished amateur artist, specialising in portraits of famous men. Soon, the banker's solid, well-ordered house had become Manby's second home, and a strange intimacy developed which was to last for nearly fifty years. There was little difference in their ages, but their relationship was not one of equality. Dawson Turner played the role of a man very much older and wiser. Manby came increasingly to rely on him for approval, encouragement, advice and money. It was a one-sided arrangement; Manby demanded, Dawson Turner gave. When he was away from Yarmouth, Manby wrote to his 'dearest friend' nearly every day—sometimes he wrote twice a day—and he always wanted something.

Dawson Turner believed in Manby. He saw in him potentialities which were far from obvious at the beginning of their friendship. He did his best to direct and to guide; he tried to inject a little reality into Manby's uncontrolled enthusiasms, and when, as he nearly always did, he failed, he was there to pick up the pieces after the inevitable disaster.

News of the victory at Trafalgar was brought to Yarmouth by coach. At first there was jubilation, with bonfires blazing, and strangers embracing in the streets. The mood changed abruptly when it was learnt that Nelson had died in the battle. A shocked disbelief was followed by an overwhelming sense of loss. A wave of hysterical grief engulfed the town. To Manby, the death of Nelson had an especial significance, personal and sharply poignant. He had followed the heroic career of his boyhood friend with pride and a feeling of proprietorship. He had felt himself in a mystical way to be part of Nelson's achievements. Now, in an atmosphere of universal mourning, while plans were being made for a funeral on an unprecedented scale, he was brought face to face with the truth. He was middle-aged, and had done nothing that was of any account. If he were to die, no flags would be lowered, no rough sailors would weep unashamedly in the streets. While Nelson had lived, the conviction that he, too, was marked for fame and honour had not faltered. Now a dreadful doubt possessed him.

Later in life Manby always claimed it was the death of Nelson which inspired him to devote himself to the saving of life from shipwreck. In fact, the need for some means of assisting vessels foundering on a lee shore had been in his mind since his fearful experience on the Arklow Bank, and had been confirmed by the succession of wrecks he had witnessed a short distance from Yarmouth beach.

Between Yarmouth and Lowestoft, parallel to the shore and about 150 yards out, there was, and no doubt still is, a ridge of sand some sixty miles long. Ships stranded on this bank in a storm were almost certainly doomed. There was an exceptionally severe gale on a night in February 1807. When it subsided, and the morning tide had left its debris, Yarmouth beach was strewn with corpses. The total number of bodies washed up was 144, and of these sixty-seven had been aboard the gun-brig *Snipe*. The brig, loaded with French prisoners of war, and a number of women and children, foundered on the sandbank less than a hundred yards out. She was close enough for the cries of those on board to be heard, but, as Manby wrote, 'as distant in effect as if she had struck a rock in the middle of the Atlantic Sea'.[5]

Manby spent the night watching the vain struggle to get a line to the *Snipe*. An attempt with a boat ended in disaster when the boat capsized and the boatman, entangled in the rope he was carrying, was strangled. The main effort was concentrated on the use of what was known as Winn's Stick.[6] This was a bamboo rod two feet long and weighted at one end with lead. A line was secured to the other end, and the idea was to throw the stick over the ship and thus deliver the line. In ideal conditions, a strong man could throw the stick a considerable distance; but with a gale force wind blowing inshore, and the line heavy with water, human muscle power was not enough. As Manby saw the repeated, fruitless attempts to throw the stick, it came to him that the answer was to shoot the line from a gun. From that moment his life was changed. His destiny had been revealed; he was to be the man whom generations of sailors would bless as a saviour.

Manby immediately started experimenting at the barracks, using a small cannon. Every time, the rope attached to the shot was burnt through by the fierce heat generated at the moment of explosion. The problem seemed insoluble, and was firmly pronounced to be so by a large number of experts, real and self-appointed. Manby, they said, was chasing the impossible—the lodestone, the perpetual motion, of gunnery.

For a time he gave up his experiments with guns, and constructed a machine based on the ancient ballista, but this proved too cumbersome and hardly more effective than Winn's bamboo stick. He returned to gunpowder, convinced that it was by this means, or not at all, that his great humanitarian object could be realised.

He was no longer seen strutting along the quay, or displaying the latest thing in waistcoats at the Assembly Rooms. The town became accustomed to the boom of cannon-fire from the barracks. It was diverting to spend an idle hour watching the little inventor and his bewildered soldier assistants at work, carefully coiling the rope so that it would play out freely, solemnly fixing it to the shot, taking aim at some distant trees before igniting the powder. And then the flash and bang of the explosion—and the rope still neatly coiled and motionless on the ground.

All through the spring and early summer of 1807 the experiments went on. Invariably they failed. The rope always burnt through at its junction with the shot. Chemical impregnation proved useless, while chains were either too heavy or broke too easily. It was essential to retain the lightness and pliability of the line, and at the same time, render its termination virtually indestructible from fire. 'I suffered,' Manby wrote of this period, 'ridicule, pity and contempt; but also encouragement from those noble and generous minds not tinctured with envy.'[7]

The Navy's corporate mind was certainly tinctured. Manby's efforts on behalf of sailors were regarded as an impertinence; but there were individual naval men who showed a sympathetic interest, and one, a Captain Burlton,[8] suggested the use of leather to join the rope to the shot. This proved to be the breakthrough. Hide was light and flexible, and when tightly plaited, tough enough to resist the heat of the explosion.

In August that year, Manby was ready to give a public demonstration of his apparatus. He submitted plans to the Suffolk Humane Society, who invited all pilots, seafarers and other interested parties to an exhibition on a wild part of the coast near Lowestoft. These trials proved beyond doubt that Manby with his small mortar cannon could successfully project a line considerable distances. The Society awarded him a medal—the first of a large collection—but there was a big gap still to be bridged between throwing the line and actually bringing survivors ashore.

At this stage, Manby's idea was that the line should be used to take out a heavier rope by means of which a boat could be hauled backwards and forwards between the stranded ship and the beach.

The theory was attractive; in practice it was unlikely to work, for the same reasons that prevented the wrecked crew launching their own boat. In a storm an open boat would almost certainly capsize. To overcome this problem, Manby designed and constructed an unsinkable boat. The principle was simple, and has remained unchanged to this day. It was to fix fore and aft and under the gunwales a series of buoyancy chambers. Manby improvised these from small wooden casks used to import limes. Sealed with pitch, these casks kept the boat afloat even when it was completely filled with water.

Up to this time, opposition to Manby's work had consisted mainly in passive derision. The invention of an unsinkable boat, however, aroused an active hatred of extraordinary intensity. It was now the ordinary working people, particularly the fishermen and boatmen, who were against him. He was no longer the harmlessly eccentric little gentleman at the barracks, amusing himself with bits of rope and gunpowder. He was transformed into a fiend who was threatening their livelihood, if not their actual lives. To an innate resentment of any sort of change was added the conviction that an unsinkable boat, by making sea-going safer and easier, would detract from the value of their labours and the mystery of their craft. Less reasonable, but to superstitious minds more powerful, was the fear of supernatural reprisals. It was believed, and in many primitive parts of the world is still believed, that the sea was a demon god, only to be placated with human sacrifice. A dreadful vengeance must inevitably follow if Manby were allowed to rob the sea of its victims. Salvage, too, played an important part in the economy of the coast. The bodies and cargo washed ashore from wrecks were a valuable source of income, so valuable that wrecks were often deliberately engineered. Altogether, it was plain to the simple people of the east coast that Manby was intent upon their ruin.

The menace was discussed at secret meetings, and the conclusion reached that the most effective way of dealing with Manby was to

drown him. It was known that Manby could not swim; if, therefore, he could be somehow deposited in the sea, well away from
shore, he would be unlikely to survive. An opportunity to carry
out this design occurred when Manby announced that he was
ready to demonstrate his unsinkable boat. A party of boatmen, all
strong swimmers, presented themselves at the barracks and
respectfully volunteered their services. Manby, unaware of their
true motives, innocently accepted.

The demonstration took place in September off Yarmouth
beach. A large crowd gathered to watch what promised to be a
first class entertainment. The atmosphere was that of a sporting
event, with bookmakers doing a brisk business in wagers for
and against the boat sinking. Sinking was odds-on favourite,
and those in the conspiracy to drown Manby found it difficult to get a respectable price on what they imagined to be a
certainty.

The boat was launched. The crew consisted of Manby, the
murderous boatmen and Manby's tailor. No one quite knew why
the tailor was there. The first part of the experiment, filling the
boat with water, was carried out successfully. The boat, although
completely waterlogged, did not sink. The next stage was to take
it out to sea, to show how, even in this condition, it could still be
navigated.

A quarter of a mile out from shore, as they began to swirl
in the strong current from Ness Point, the boatmen stood up,
shouting: 'We want to see if she will overset!' They then started
to sway violently from side to side in unison. They ignored
Manby's frantic protests, and continued their shouting and sway-
ing until the boat turned turtle and tipped them all into the sea.
The boatmen immediately struck out for the shore, leaving
Manby and the tailor, who couldn't swim either, floundering in
the current. One boatman, whose conscience was more sensitive
than his fellows', returned to grab the tailor, but Manby was left,
according to plan, to drown. Somehow he managed to keep

Manby's canvas sling, forerunner of the breeches buoy

'Captain Manby's method of conveying the people on shore':
engraving after Sartorius

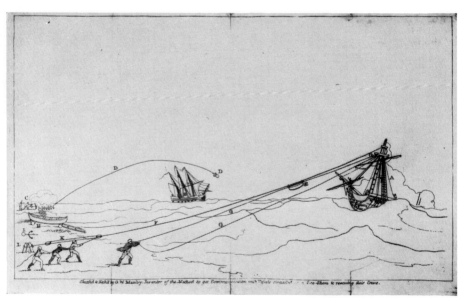

Manby's explanatory drawing of the apparatus

afloat, proving, he said, that anyone could swim if they had to, until he was reached by two heroic spectators who plunged to his rescue.[9]

This second unsuccessful attempt on his life merely served to harden Manby's stubborn determination. He was now a man utterly dedicated to one purpose—to prove the value of his apparatus, and then to have it established all round the coasts of Great Britain. But there were obstacles to overcome, very much more formidable than the prejudice of a few ignorant boatmen. The Admiralty, without whom little progress could be made, refused to take Manby seriously. To them, Manby's invention was a soldier's toy, of no practical value, and the fact that the Board of Ordnance appeared to be sponsoring the experiments did not incline them to a more favourable opinion.

The Board had supported Manby from the outset. They had provided him with guns, ammunition and powder; they had allowed him soldier assistants, and had arranged the continual leave of absence from his proper duties that the experiments entailed. By command of the Board, Manby gave a series of demonstrations before a committee of field officers of the Artillery. From a wharf at Woolwich Arsenal, he successfully projected ropes over a ship lying in the Thames. The Committee's report was favourable, but artillery officers had no power to move the Admiralty. They could only suggest that the question of practicability be submitted to officers of the Royal Navy.

It was now February 1808—almost exactly a year since the wreck of the *Snipe*. Once again there was fog and foul weather, and any night a ship might ground on the sandbank off Yarmouth beach. Manby was well prepared. He had made a cart to transport the mortar, and baskets for the ropes which could be carried on a man's back. His unsinkable boat was positioned close to the beach, and a soldier was detailed to patrol the shore every night, keeping a look-out for vessels in distress.

During the night of February 12th there was one of the worst storms anyone could remember. Manby did not wait to be summoned. He joined his sentry out in the icy wind, where great waves were thundering on the beach. He felt convinced that this was the night his apparatus would be tried in earnest. His premonition proved to be correct. In the early hours, the little brig *Elizabeth*, dismasted and blown inexorably inshore, grounded on the sandbank. Manby dashed back to the barracks, aroused his party of soldiers, loaded them with powder, shot and baskets of rope and then helped to drag the mortar on its improvised carriage down to the beach.

Dawn was breaking, and in the murk of the storm the crew of the *Elizabeth* could just be made out, clinging desperately to the broken rigging. Manby had drilled his party well; each man knew exactly what to do. First, the mortar was anchored by means of iron-tipped staves driven into the sand, then it was primed, and loaded with a barbed shot, fitted with an eye to which 200 fathoms of line was secured with plaited leather thongs. Within half an hour of sighting the wreck, Manby was ready for firing. He had foreseen the difficulty of touching off the powder in the wind and rain, and he had invented a chemical igniter for the purpose. It worked the first time, and as the gun fired the coiled rope simultaneously came to life and leapt towards the sea, playing out so fast it appeared simply to vanish from the basket.

Soon the rope sagged and fell. The shot had landed; the vital question was, where had it landed? Manby had fired almost blind into a gale. The brig was a relatively small target, and mortar fire was, at the best of times, erratic and unpredictable in direction. They waited, watching the inert rope for some sign that human hands had grasped the other end. In the howling wind and freezing rain, a crowd had now gathered on the beach, for word had reached the town of the drama that was taking place, but, looking at the rope trailing lifelessly into the surf, it seemed they had left their warm beds for nothing.

And then, in a series of spasmodic jerks, the rope began to

move. Painfully, what was left in the basket inched its way into the sea. As it moved, Manby and his crew knotted on the heavy rope, and while this was being hauled out, they dragged the unsinkable boat down to the edge of the sea. Now it was light enough to see the men on the brig quite clearly. The crowd waved to them frantically, shouting into the wind: 'Haul away! Haul away!' The heavy rope, now fixed to the stern of the boat, lifted as it took the strain. The boat slid into the surf, bucking wildly as it met the breakers head-on. It stayed afloat, and as the men on the brig heaved, Manby's party on the shore played out the remaining rope, by means of which, when the sailors had scrambled on board, they hauled it back.

There were seven men in the boat when it was at last dragged up on to the beach. They were terrified, exhausted, frozen and soaked to the skin; but they were all alive. The crowd pressed round them, eager to welcome and assist—all except the man without whose efforts they would have arrived on the beach with the next tide as battered corpses. Manby had moved away, overcome with emotion. He fell on his knees in the sand and thanked God. He was crying like a child.

The rescued seamen were taken up to the barracks, given dry clothing, hot rum and finally beds. But before Manby allowed him to sleep, the master of the *Elizabeth*, John Prouting, was given paper and pen and asked to write a testimonial. Manby knew the speed with which human gratitude dissipated; he was aware, too, that there were a number of reasons, professional and commercial, why the rescued mariners might decide to deny they had been assisted. Manby wanted documentary evidence now, before the reaction set in and before the men he had snatched from death could be reached by crafty advice. Laboriously, the captain certified that he and his crew had been saved by Manby's apparatus, and that in his opinion, they could not possibly have been saved by any other means. He was fully convinced that the invention of throwing a rope to vessels stranded on a lee shore was of the utmost consequence and importance to a maritime country, besides being interesting to the world at large.[10]

Despite the unqualified success of his first rescue, Manby was not wholly satisfied. In his heart, he knew that too much had depended on luck, and on the fact that there had been only seven men on the brig, all experienced seamen. A spectator on the beach had said to him: 'Your plan seems only adapted when a boat is at hand.' Manby had refuted this criticism energetically, saying: 'Excuse me, they have a line by which, if they cut away the shot, they may be drawn from the wreck in safety by people on shore.' But the doubt had been sown in his mind. The system did depend on the availability of a boat, and there would often be circumstances where a boat, even if available, could not be launched. And then, even supposing it were possible to drag people to land on the end of the rope without drowning them, what about women, children and those who were injured?

Manby went back to work to devise some alternative to a boat for bringing people to land. His solution to the problem was a crude prototype of the present day breeches buoy. In its original form, this was a canvas sling in which a man could be transported along an aerial rope by means of pulleys. Manby himself was the first person to travel by this means from the mainmast of a ship to the shore, when he gave a demonstration before the Admiral of the Port of Yarmouth. Another refinement to the apparatus which he developed was a form of star shot which could be fired at night to discover the position of the wreck and enable the mortar to be aimed accurately. Then, so that the wrecked crew would be able to see the approach of the line and where it landed, he produced a tracer shell. All this experimental work, apart from the assistance in materials and men he received from the Board of Ordnance, was at his own expense.

Manby had hopes of recouping his expenses, and eventually of making a profit, by selling his apparatus privately. He produced an illustrated advertisement, explaining in detail the method of using the apparatus, and appended a price list. He did this, he said, so that 'the benevolent intentions of such persons who view the importance of seamen's lives in a NATIONAL light' would not be discouraged by 'the apprehension of hearty expense'. A small mortar, with shot ready strapped for immediate use, he undertook to supply for £7. 17. 6. All other materials he would engage to supply at the cost of a few pounds. He sent hundreds of copies of this circular to Lord Lieutenants, magistrates, shipowners and private philanthropists living in coastal areas all around the country. There were no orders. It was clearly hopeless to rely on private benevolence. Private individuals, in any event, however willing they might be, could not establish the kind of national life-saving service that Manby envisaged. This must be organised and financed by the government, and placed under the direction of a man of outstanding capability who would be adequately rewarded. There was no doubt in his own mind that such a man was available.

He obtained a period of extended leave, borrowed more money from Dawson Turner and took the coach for London. The Barrack Sergeant, left in charge, was given orders to pack the mortar, the shot, the ropes and the rest of the equipment, ready to be dispatched at a moment's notice.

Manby campaigned in London with indefatigable energy. He lobbied Members of Parliament, pestered Ministers, petitioned Royalty; an unceasing flow of letters, pamphlets and addresses issued from his lodgings in Suffolk Street. The slightest sign of encouragement he interpreted as unqualified approval, a polite word of praise he magnified into the most fulsome compliment. He did succeed in arousing public interest. The time was propitious. The country depended for its survival upon a continued mastery of the sea. Sailors' lives, in normal times of little account, had for the moment assumed a real and a sentimental value. The simplicity of Manby's apparatus helped. It was something everyone could understand with no great effort. It was also theatrical;

Manby's demonstrations combined the thrills of a circus act and a firework display, and they always drew large crowds.

His most ambitious and successful performance took place in Hyde Park, and among the spectators were the Duke of York and his brother the Duke of Kent. Manby, using his tracer shell, threw a line over the Serpentine to a distant tree, in the branches of which an assistant was lodged, as though in the rigging of a ship. With one end of the line secured to the tree, and the other to a gun-tackle purchase, the canvas cot was sent out and, amid cheers from the crowd, the assistant travelled through the air over the lake to join Manby on the bank.

It was a convincing performance, and when it was over Manby was summoned to the presence of the royal brothers.

'I see the importance of your invention,' said the Duke of Kent. 'I anticipate, and am convinced, that immense good will result from it, to this and other nations, and I am sure your country will be grateful to you for it.'[11]

The Duke of York said nothing. He was, perhaps, too pre-occupied with other, more urgent matters. In a few weeks a huge scandal was due to break over his head when he would be accused, alongside his ex-mistress, of corruption. Manby's contraption might rescue sailors; it could not rescue him.

The Lords of the Admiralty continued to remain aloof and, influenced no doubt by their advice, the acting Prime Minister, Spencer Perceval, was unenthusiastic. He did not feel that Manby's device merited the expenditure of public money at this stage. But pressure from all factions forced his hand. He agreed to the setting up of a Committee to study Manby's scheme.

At this point Manby's hopes received a severe jolt by the revelation that something very like his apparatus had been invented nearly twenty years before by a man called John Bell.[12] To make matters worse, Bell had been given an award for it by the Society for the Encouragement of Arts. Bell was dead, and could not champion his own cause; but the Society was quick to take up the cudgels on his behalf. A pamphlet[13] appeared with a full description of Bell's invention, and a statement which, although not mentioning him by name, was clearly aimed at discrediting Manby.

'A Publicity having been given,' the Society's statement ran, 'to some experiments for the preserving of lives from shipwreck by means of a rope attached to a shell thrown from a mortar, the Society think it incumbent upon them to remind the public that so far back as the year 1792, a bounty of fifty guineas was given to John Bell, then a Sergeant, afterwards Lieutenant of the Royal Regiment of Artillery, for his invention of throwing a rope on shore by means of a shell fired from a mortar on board a vessel in distress.'

Bell's proposal, the reverse of Manby's, had been to equip ships with line-throwing guns; yet the actual apparatus, as the illustrations in the pamphlet emphasised, was strikingly similar. There was no question of illegality; no patent rights were involved; anyone was entitled to tie a piece of rope to a cannon-ball and fire it. The dispute was about who deserved the kudos and reward for applying the idea to the saving of life from shipwreck. The Society was willing to concede that Manby might have hit upon the idea independently, but if he persisted in claiming to be the original inventor, then he was a plagiarist and a liar.

Manby did persist. He suddenly remembered that as a youth of eighteen, he had constructed a small mortar and had attempted to shoot a line over the tower of Downham church. He had broken a window in the process, and the rector had made a great to-do. There were people, he said, still living at Downham who could vouch for this incident. He did not explain why it was only now, after Bell's prior claim had been raised, that he remembered it.

Manby was terrified that these attacks might prejudice the Parliamentary Committee against him. He fought back desperately. 'Feeling my veracity is at stake,' he declared, 'I consider myself called upon to boldly and unhesitatingly claim my own, and not subject myself either while I live, or after my death, to the despicable suspicion of dishonourable fraud.'

Whatever Bell might, or might not, have invented or proposed, he had never rescued anyone, while Manby already had seven lives to his credit. The vital difference between them was that of failure and success; or, as Manby put it: 'The difference between the plan submitted by Bell, and that brought in by myself, is the difference that is often found to exist between a specious theoretical idea, and a confirmed practical truth.'[14]

The issue was never finally resolved. Bell's supporters did not press home their attacks; they contented themselves with sporadic sniping, which was more irritating than dangerous. The Committee decided that although Manby might have been superseded as far as the basic idea went, the credit for its successful application was his alone. The Committee awarded Manby £2,000, and recommended that he be made responsible for conducting a survey of the coast, to report where permanent stations for his apparatus should be established.[15]

Manby was delirious with joy. He saw himself heading a new department for the preservation of life at sea, and the prevention of shipwreck. Such an appointment would doubtless carry with it an honour which could scarcely be less than a knighthood. 'So now, thank Heaven,' he wrote to Dawson Turner, 'my fortune is made.'[16]

It did, indeed, seem to be so at the time.

3

WHEN MANBY SET out on his survey of the coast, he did not expect that he would ever return to the mundane duties of Barrack Master. Long before the survey was complete, he was confident there would be a new Department of State for the Preservation of Life from Shipwreck with himself at its head. Meanwhile, he made the most of his position as Special Commissioner, directly responsible to the Home Secretary.

Manby started his survey in Norfolk, and worked his way up the coast to the Firth of Forth. He progressed with ambassadorial panache through the towns and villages, delighting in the flattering attention he received, the unaccustomed deference of local dignitaries and landowners. His exalted role as envoy of the House of Commons cost a good deal of money to maintain. He was obliged to dress for the part and to entertain rather lavishly. He regarded these as essential items of expense, and expected to be reimbursed. Unfortunately, the bureaucrats in Whitehall did not agree; there was, in fact, an irreconcilable difference of opinion between them and Manby, regarding the importance of his mission. Manby's claims for expenses were invariably queried.[1] The Home Office was prepared to pay for necessary travel, moderate lodgings and daily subsistence. They refused to pay for silk waistcoats and dinner parties.

Manby saw his job in fundamentally different terms to the officials in London. He did not look upon himself, as they did, merely as a surveyor. He was convinced that Parliament had entrusted him with the great task of converting whole communities to the noble idea behind the prosaic mortar, shot and rope. He discovered he had a talent for evangelism. He held public meetings; he gave lectures. Along the lonely coast there was little entertainment, and Manby's lectures were always well attended and heartily applauded. Although he prepared with great care, sometimes working all night, he gave the impression of spontaneity. He could drop his notes and take his hearers into his confidence; he could inspire them with a sense of his own obsessive sincerity. Moreover, in advance of his times, he realised the power of visual demonstration. The highlight of his lectures was an actual rescue staged with working models. Whitehall did not regard any of this as a proper expense, and Manby had to foot the bills himself. When he ran out of money, which did not take very long, Dawson Turner paid.

It took Manby two years to reach Leith, by which time he had made out a case for 170 stations for his apparatus. He planned to continue his survey up into the Highlands, and then down the west coast. But by now a change of government had taken place, the economic situation had deteriorated still further and Manby was a saving that could readily be made. He was told that his services would no longer be required, and that he could resume his duties as Barrack Master. The new Department upon which Manby had set such high hopes was forgotten, and the future responsibility for the life-saving apparatus given to the Board of Customs. The Board took over all the existing equipment, much of which was Manby's own property, and guarded it as closely as contraband. Manby, it seemed, was deliberately excluded. It was made clear immediately that any interference on his part would be firmly dealt with.

The government had placed orders for 1,000 mortars, but with the armament factories already unable to meet the demands of the Army and Navy, this was little more than a gesture. By 1815 only forty-five sets of equipment had been delivered, and many of these were useless because they were incomplete, or soon became useless because there was no one to operate or maintain them.[2] The volunteers who had been recruited to take charge of the stations—it might be the local schoolmaster, sometimes it was the parson—tended to lose interest when they found it difficult to get suitable assistants, and more difficult still to get the money to pay them. It was only in Norfolk and Suffolk, where Manby, despite the obstruction of the Board of Customs, managed to retain some control, that the system worked efficiently. For every life saved in the rest of the country, eleven were saved in Norfolk and Suffolk, and this remarkable success rate was due almost entirely to Manby's personal efforts.

The shabby treatment Manby had received from his own government was mitigated in some degree by the gratitude of foreign countries, whose subjects had been saved by his apparatus. Manby was steadily acquiring a large collection of presentation medals, inscribed with a variety of languages. He was pathetically proud of his medals, and wore them pinned to his inadequate chest on every possible occasion.[3]

In the winter of 1812, while Manby was in Scotland, he was appalled by the number of people who were being drowned when they fell through the ice that covered the lakes, lochs and rivers. When seventeen lives were lost in one day on a lake near Edinburgh, in full view of hundreds of spectators, Manby decided to do something about it.

He designed a rope with a noose distended by whalebone, to throw over anyone whose head and shoulders were above the surface, and a grapple to drag clear anyone who was trapped under the ice.

The following winter, back in London, Manby improved and expanded his inventions. For occasions when the ice was too rotten to bear the weight of rescuers, he designed a sectional ladder, bouyant at one end, and a sectional rod, terminating in a grappling iron to fish for bodies, but with barbs that would not penetrate too deeply into the flesh. If the ice would not even support the ladder, there was a sledge-boat made of wickerwork, which could be propelled by a spiked pole and would accommodate two men.[4]

The system had a gratifying success. At one period sixteen people were saved in three days from the canal in St James's Park, and this encouraged Manby to apply for the gold medal which the Royal Society of Arts was offering for a cheap, portable drag for taking up, with least injury, the bodies of persons sunk under water. Although Manby was the only candidate, his application met some determined opposition. He had offended the Society by claiming to be the sole inventor of the line-throwing mortar. 'Much enmity,' he wrote, 'was displayed against me, which betrayed the Committee into great warmth of temper and irregularity of proceeding.' It was proposed to award him merely the silver medal, but 'some persons of reasoning and liberal minds, detecting the impropiety of this, prolonged the meeting until 11 p.m. when business must be concluded.'[5]

Manby retaliated with a pamphlet,[6] attacking the Committee as 'persons neither exalted by rank, nor that dignity of mind which flows from a liberal education. With such persons, prejudice and ignorance will enter, and, left to their uncontrolled guidance, the Society will soon have an operation the reverse of its intention.'

Having published this diatribe, Manby again applied for the gold medal. This time, he did not even qualify for the silver.

Manby's wife died in her guilty exile in 1814. Manby decided to marry again; but this time he was determined to choose with care. After his disastrous experience with a passionate, headstrong beauty, he looked for a gentle, docile woman, who would be content with a subservient, domestic role. This was one basic requirement. But there were others. He needed a wife of breeding, for there was no doubt in his mind, despite temporary setbacks, that she would have to take an exalted place in the world. At the very least, he was searching for a potential Lady Manby. It would also be a great advantage if his wife had money, or, at any rate, the prospects of money.

These were stringent specifications, but it seemed to Manby that Sophia Gooch satisfied them. She was the daughter of a wealthy squire, Sir Thomas Gooch, with a substantial estate in Suffolk.[7] Sir Thomas was an old man at the time Dawson Turner introduced Manby to him. He raised no objections to Manby's suit; Sophia, in any event, was over forty, and the match probably seemed the best that could reasonably be expected.

There were other members of the Gooch family, however, who did not approve, in particular the heir to the baronetcy, young Thomas Sherlock Gooch. He regarded Manby as a mountebank, a penniless adventurer whose only motive in courting Sophia was to get hold of her money.

While his father was alive, there was little he could do except insult Manby on every possible occasion; but when he came into the title, as he did a few years after the marriage had taken place in 1818, he carried on a relentless campaign of vilification, designed to prevent Manby from getting his hands on a penny of the Gooch fortune, and to ostracise him from county society.

The success he achieved was due in a large measure to Manby's own behaviour, which gave verisimilitude to the slanders spread so thickly about him. In particular, his treatment of Sophia was something his staunchest friends found it difficult to excuse or justify. The way he neglected his wife became the standard scandal of Yarmouth. There were times when she was actually on the point of starvation, and yet Manby genuinely believed that he was a devoted and attentive husband. He was bewildered and outraged at the charges brought against him.

Altogether, it was a peculiar marriage. Sophia was as shy and self-effacing as Manby was brash and pertinacious. She could not follow him in his obsessive pursuit of fame and glory. She could not share, or even understand, his absurd hopes and dreams. She was completely undemanding and accepted her background role with uncomplaining resignation. Manby's increasingly complicated affairs caused him to disregard his duties and obligations both as a Barrack Master and as a husband. It was comforting to know that his job and his wife were there, a refuge he could fall back on when things became difficult; but his heart and his ambition, which were for him the same thing, lay in a wider, more important world than the barrack square and the domestic hearth. Yarmouth became a place he occasionally visited; the long-suffering Barrack Sergeant grew accustomed to a position of sole charge, and it was left to Dawson Turner to look after Mrs Manby and to pay the tradesmen's bills.

The Customs had taken over the saving of life from shipwreck, and it was only in winter that people fell through ice; but there was always fire to challenge a man who, late in life, had adopted salvation as a career.

At this period of history, fires were so frequent they had come to be accepted as a natural and inescapable hazard of life. Fire precautions were virtually non-existent, while fire-fighting arrangements were haphazard and hopelessly inefficient. There was a law requiring every parish to provide a fire engine under the charge of a constable. Nobody took this very seriously, and even when the engines existed, they usually became useless with neglect.

The government was content to leave the business of putting

out fires to private enterprise. In practice, this meant that it was almost solely the concern of the big fire insurance companies, whose only object was to save money by reducing claims. They had to balance the commercial advantage of putting a fire out against that of letting it burn. It was only in the big cities that it was worth while for the companies to maintain a fire-fighting organisation, and even in the big cities it was done in the cheapest possible way.

Apart from the fact that the Fire Offices were only interested in premises belonging to their own customers, the untrained, poorly paid firemen, with their crude, inefficient equipment, were quite incapable of dealing with a well-established fire. In these circumstances, it was vital for the fire to be detected, and the alarm given, in its early stages. Manby attended a meeting in the City at which the idea of a fire patrol was put forward. The proposal was that each Fire Office should provide two men, armed with a flambeau and an axe, to patrol the streets of London all night, keeping a look-out for incipient fires.

Manby immediately perceived the limitations of this scheme. How much more effective the patrols would be, he reasoned, if, instead of merely giving the alarm, they were themselves equipped to deal with small fires on the spot. To enable them to do this, Manby produced the most remarkable and original invention of his career—a portable fire extinguisher. This was a copper cylinder, two feet long and eight inches in diameter, with a capacity of four gallons. It was three-quarters filled with a solution of water and antiphlogistic chemicals, after which compressed air was pumped in and trapped by means of a valve. When the valve was released, a powerful jet of the liquid was forced out through the nozzle. These extinguishers were light enough for a man to lift and carry for short distances, and the proposed patrolmen could easily take a couple about with them on a small hand-cart.[8]

There was a fortune to be made from Manby's new invention, but nearly a century was to pass before anyone grasped the opportunity. Manby himself did not realise the vast commercial potential of his idea; certainly he did not foresee the present day aerosol boom, and the application of his principle to a bewildering variety of liquids. Manby was not a business man; his ambition was not to make money, but to be regarded as a great public benefactor. The rewards he craved for were fame and honour; wealth was a secondary consideration which he expected to flow naturally from the gratitude of his countrymen.

The scheme for fire patrols equipped with Manby's extinguishers never progressed beyond the talking stage. It was discussed at public meetings, it gave rise to committees. The Lord Mayor favoured the idea, and so, in principle, did the insurance companies. But no one was actually prepared to finance it, or even to reimburse Manby for the expense of his prototype extinguisher. Manby's load of debt increased alarmingly, and his appeals for help to Dawson Turner became more frantic and frequent. It was clearly time for another voyage.

The opportunity which arose to escape from his creditors, his boring duties and irksome domesticity, could hardly have been more opportune, or more unlikely. Early in 1821 he sailed for the Arctic in the whaling ship *Baffin*.

4

WHALE FISHERY, AT one time a prosperous industry, had gradually
been falling into decline and had reached a point where it was
scarcely worth while to send ships to the Arctic. Not only had
over-fishing made whales harder and more expensive to catch,
but whale products were also less in demand and lower in price.
The only way, it seemed, in which whale fishery could survive as
a commercial proposition was for more whales to be captured at
a lower cost.

The traditional fishing methods were primitive, barbarous and
extremely dangerous. They were also inefficient. When the great
mammals surfaced for air, they were attacked at close quarters by
parties of men in small boats. It often took hours of vicious
lunging with hand-held harpoons and lances to kill a whale; many
escaped, and frequently it was the whalers themselves who perished.
Few whaling ships returned to port without at least one coffin
hanging over the stern.

There had been half-hearted attempts to replace the hand-held harpoon with one fired from a gun, but they had not been successful. The guns had proved to have a limited range, and the harpoons fired from them invariably caused a large wound when they entered the whale and retracted too easily. It was, however, the resistance of the harpooners, rather than the shortcomings of the gun, which inhibited its use and development. Harpooners were highly skilled, highly privileged and highly paid. They formed a small, closely guarded guild. They were tough and independent, and allowed no outside interference. A man could be admitted to their ranks only after a long, hard and dangerous apprenticeship, working his way up through the inferior grades of rope-coiler and boatsteerer. Harpooners looked upon themselves as the elite of the Arctic; mere sailors, whether they were deck-hands or Masters, they treated with disdain. These men had set their faces against the harpoon-gun. They reasoned, and history has to a great extent proved them to have been right, that a successful harpoon-gun would mark the end of their special status and undermine the high value of their services. Any man who could fire a gun would be able to call himself a harpooner.

Despite past failures, and the determined opposition of the harpooners, the President of the Board of Trade was convinced that the future of the industry depended on an efficient harpoon-gun, and Manby, with his unique experience in projecting ropes, was asked to suggest improvements to the existing apparatus. Entirely at his own expense, Manby set to work and in a few months produced the prototype of a redesigned harpoon-gun which was extremely ingenious, and appeared to solve the problems of range and retraction. The gun had many original features, the most revolutionary of which was the percussion lock, while the harpoon had spring-loaded, non-retractable barbs. In practice shots at the barracks, a harpoon from Manby's gun could penetrate a two-inch board, point-blank, at a range of thirty yards.[1]

The harpoon, whether hand-held or gun fired, was of use only as a preliminary operation, to secure the whale on the end of a rope and prevent its escape. The actual killing was accomplished by stabbing it with iron-tipped lances. This was the most dangerous and disgusting part of the business, and to obviate it, Manby designed an oblong shell, detonating on impact, which would kill the whale outright by exploding inside the viscera.[2]

Manby's invention of a lock which fired by percussion and an oblong shell which detonated on impact had a significance which went far beyond the killing of whales. They could also be used for killing people, but, at the time, he had no conception of their military importance. Ironically, the man who had dedicated himself to saving human life was laying the foundations of modern warfare.

It was not easy to persuade the owners of a whaling vessel to allow Manby to make a voyage to try out his new devices. Owners were reluctant to risk offending their harpooners, while few Masters would agree to add an elderly amateur gunner to their already formidable burdens. Arctic sailors as a class were rough, hard-bitten men, whose only motive for enduring the dangers and hardships of their voyages was to make enough money for an orgy of drinking and whoring when they came back to port. They were usually brilliant seamen—they had to be in order to survive— but they did not possess sensitive feelings, cultured intellects, polite manners or scientific curiosity.

Captain Scoresby,[3] Master of the *Baffin*, was a rare exception. He was a gentleman and a scientist, soft-spoken, highly moral and deeply religious. Although he was only twenty-nine, he was already distinguished for his work on navigation and the earth's magnetism, and he had adopted whaling because it provided an opportunity to pursue his researches, and also from a desire to explore the virtually unknown continent of Greenland. In particular, he was interested in the West, or so called Lost Greenland, which, several centuries before, had been colonised by Christian missionaries from Norway. Neither Captain Scoresby nor the owners of the *Baffin* were exactly enthusiastic; nevertheless, they did agree that Manby could join the ship, and, if the opportunity arose, try out his new gun.

In the middle of March, Manby set off for Liverpool. To the Barrack Sergeant he entrusted the running of the barracks; to Dawson Turner the care of his domestic responsibilities, which now, besides a wife, included two young men. These were the brothers Joy,[4] the sons of the guard of the Yarmouth mail coach. They both possessed a remarkable natural talent for painting, and Manby had taken them under his wing, giving them a room at the barracks as a studio. He asked Dawson Turner to keep an eye on his two protégés, and 'encourage them to confine themselves to marine subjects, attentively to look, imitate and copy that noble picture always before them—*that of nature*—from the room where I have placed them'. He also hoped his friend would look after them if he did not return from the Arctic—a possibility which was far from remote.[5]

Manby was fifty-six. Quite apart from the dangers inherent in the voyage, the hardships and the temperatures might well prove fatal to a man of his age and uncertain health. Manby was fully aware of the risks. He made his will, which he sent to Dawson Turner 'to correct any little inaccuracies', and asked that should the worst happen, a simple stone be placed in Denver church as a record of the event.

In Liverpool, Manby stayed with Captain Scoresby and his wife. The Captain greatly impressed Manby, who thought him one of the most extraordinary men he had ever met. 'Considering he is only 29,' he wrote to Dawson Turner, 'one of the most extraordinary men of his age. I feel in his society as if I know nothing.'

Scoresby fired Manby's imagination by telling him that on this voyage he hoped to penetrate regions known only from conjecture, and where the foot of man had never trod. The prospect was romantic and exciting; Manby immediately put in a request that his foot be the first.

Scoresby, for his part, found Manby's bouncing confidence infectious. In a letter to the *Baffin*'s owners, he wrote: 'I have seen the apparatus which I think promises well. It is original, and as far as I can judge, may be useful, not only in ordinary cases, but what is of equal or greater importance in situations where the ordinary practice will not avail.' He added, however, a note of scientific caution: 'Captain M. is sanguine, and not without reason; but we who have not so much at stake (as regards the success of the invention) are apt to calculate on possibilities perhaps on the safest side.'[6]

The *Baffin*[7] sailed from the Mersey at the beginning of April 1821, and did not return until September. From almost every point of view the voyage was a failure, bedevilled by bad luck, foul weather and abnormal ice conditions. They only captured four whales; they did not land on Lost Greenland, and Manby did not once fire his harpoon gun.

Manby kept a journal of the voyage.[8] He wrote it with an eye to publication, padding it out with tedious zoological and geographical detail in an effort to make it a worthy scientific treatise. As an account of daily life on a whaler, and of the way the strong and contrasting personalities aboard reacted to being cooped up together for half a year in a weird, frozen world, it is disappointing. His fellow sailors remain shadowy figures, and it is only by reading between the lines that we catch tantalising glimpses of the prim, sanctimonious Captain, the tough, insolently independent harpooners, the crafty steward who watered down the grog ration and the boatsteerers who tied girls' garters to their ropes and sang outrageous songs.

From the outset, it was clear that the harpooners were in a dangerous mood. They regarded Manby's presence on board as an insult, and they made no secret of their intention to sabotage his experiments. They were equally outspoken in their criticism of the

Captain's cautious, old-maidish ways and religious mania. Prayer meetings every evening they might tolerate as a skipper's idiosyncrasy; but when Scoresby refused to allow any fishing to desecrate the Sabbath, even though a whale might be blowing right alongside, they became openly mutinous.

After they had been at sea three weeks, and had crossed the Northern Polar Circle, Scoresby, as a gesture of propitiation, invited the harpooners to dinner in his cabin. There was roast beef and plum pudding, followed by a plentiful supply of grog. The harpooners mellowed a little, and Manby judged the moment favourable to 'address them in a tone which might, if possible, remove the hostile impression which I both plainly saw, and was confidently assured, existed against my inventions'.

He was there, he told them, not from any selfish motives, but purely from a desire to benefit his country by improving whale fishing. He also wished to lessen its dangers, and to 'obviate the necessity for barbarity, which has called forth the clamorous indignation of some who possess the finer feelings of sensibility'.

The harpooners heard him in silence; this encouraged him to make a direct appeal to the man who had been allotted to him for his experiments.

'Richard Simpkin,' he said, 'you have been selected to the charge and direction of the boat appointed to try the practical utility of my gun and other apparatus. I only ask for a fair and impartial trial. It is now proper for me to state that you have been selected, as this being your first voyage in the rank of harpooner, there is less liability of your being influenced by prejudice, or obstinate adherence to old customs.'[9]

Still the harpooners said nothing; but the following morning Richard Simpkin was reported to be suffering from a mysterious indisposition, and it was not until the beginning of June that he recovered sufficiently to take Manby and his gun out to attack a whale.

Up to this time only two inferior specimens had been captured.

Unusually close-packed ice combined with hurricanes and heavy snow had kept the crew fully occupied with survival. But now, for a brief period, the weather cleared, and as they sailed, the sun shining brilliantly, into a great bay in the western ice, there seemed to be whales everywhere. Captain Scoresby, directing operations from the masthead, counted thirty-two, and amid a great uproar of excitement he ordered every available boat to be launched.

'I was ordered to as favourable spot as could be selected,' wrote Manby, 'and from which whales had just retired. Here we remained, narrowly watching for the reappearance of our destined prey.'[10]

Manby also watched narrowly the behaviour of Richard Simpkin, and he found it to be most unsatisfactory. The young harpooner was sullen and unco-operative, and seemed to be doing all he could to keep Manby out of range of a whale. When, despite Simpkin's efforts, the opportunity at last came to fire his harpoon, Manby discovered that the gun had been tampered with and 'a most disgraceful trick employed to defeat its going off'.[11]

Angry and disgusted, Manby threw in his hand. For the first, and perhaps the only time in his life, he admitted defeat. 'I determined,' he wrote, 'to take no further interest in proving the decided advantages of my gun—and wished them better success than had hitherto attended their taking fish by hand harpoon.'[12]

Manby's interest was now centred upon landing on Lost Greenland. His desire to witness the remote and long lost country, he told Dawson Turner, was not common curiosity, but because he wished to take possession of it in the name of the King, 'and when the Dominion of Greenland is named, that of Manby be preserved till the end of time'. But all Scoresby's attempts to find a landing were frustrated by the ice and fog, and finally had to be abandoned. The nearest Manby came to creating the Dominion of Manbyland was a distant view from the masthead of green, mysterious hills across an impenetrable frozen sea.

The fog and snow persisted until late July. Manby shot a

walrus and a large polar bear, but no more whales were seen, and Scoresby decided to start the difficult passage back to the open sea and home. After the fog came tremendous gales which blew the *Baffin* three hundred miles off course on to the coast of Iceland, and it was not until dawn on September 8th that the look-out shouted: 'Land right ahead!' and the hills of North Wales gradually materialised on the horizon.

For all the frustrations and hardships, Manby still regarded the voyage as one of the best parts of his life. 'The privations were infinitely greater than I expected,' he told Dawson Turner, 'and the dangers innumerable—but sailor-like, I think no more of them once passed.' Beneath the slight, frail-seeming figure was a man of action and violence, and this man had been released on the *Baffin*. He might not have revolutionised whale fishing or founded a new Dominion, but there was a deep personal satisfaction in the knowledge that his courage and his endurance had passed a formidable test.

Although his experiences had convinced Manby of the potential value of his gun, he made no further efforts to develop or exploit its possibilities. The government, too, lost interest, and it was left to the Norwegians to reap the benefit when Manby's apparatus was re-invented by Sven Foyn in 1872.

Instead of persevering with his gun, Manby squandered his energies on an absurd idea he had conceived of making Lost Greenland into a criminal colony. His scheme was to send the hundreds of persons annually condemned to death for forgery to Greenland, where 'with seasonable and adequate supply of clothing, bedding and other attentions to their comfort, health and morals, they could become useful members of society'.[13]

Another unfortunate offshoot of his voyage was a bitter quarrel with the publisher Whittaker. Whittaker had agreed to publish Manby's journal, but the arrangement was a verbal one, and the two men's recollection of the exact terms did not coincide.

Manby claimed that Whittaker had agreed that the author was to have the proceeds of the subscription copies, less expenses. Whittaker denied having said anything of the sort; but that the author was to have the proceeds, less expenses, of any copies sold *other* than the subscription copies.

Manby, who had expected to pay his debts from the sale of his book, fought desperately to establish his claim, despite the fact that the sum involved was relatively minute, only 140 copies having been sold in all. It was clear to everyone, except Manby, that Whittaker's version of the contract was more likely to be the true one. Dawson Turner, to whom Manby appealed for help, was, on this occasion, unwilling to act for him, while his lawyer, Upcott, was 'a very different man from when we last met—instead of that warm reception he used to greet me with, it was cold, and gave me very little encouragement'.[14]

Whittaker himself was always out when Manby called. Eventually, he agreed to buy the copyright, and although Manby was horrified when he heard the price offered—£35—his desperate circumstances forced him to accept.

Manby's hopes of fame and fortune from his book might have been dashed, but there was another bright prospect coming into view. The scheme for establishing a department for the saving of lives from shipwreck had been revived in Parliament, and instead of returning to Yarmouth, Manby stayed in London, lobbying for all he was worth. He printed a pamphlet listing all the lives that had been saved by his apparatus—the total was now 600—and he also made further efforts to allay the doubt that he was the original inventor of the line and mortar rescue system.

Dawson Turner's sane advice was not to place too great reliance on an appointment, but to submit a petition for an annuity, as a reward for his distinguished services. Manby tried desperately to gain an interview with Peel; but Peel proved to be an elusive man. After several days spent waiting hopefully in the great man's waiting room, Manby had to content himself with presenting an underling with a list of his services. Full of confidence, he wrote to Dawson Turner that he hoped to return to Yarmouth an independent man. Meanwhile, would his dear friend pay his taxes and honour a bill for £9 that had fallen due.

Manby's petition was presented to the House at the end of April 1823, and was referred to a Committee. 'The object of doing this,' Manby wrote to Dawson Turner, 'is not only to procure me the £400 annuity prayed for, but also to place me in a distinguished situation as head of a Department, highly honourable and profitable. I consider my fortune made.'

Whatever reward he might receive, he promised that Dawson Turner should have power of attorney, so that his greatest wish could be realised—that of paying every farthing he owed. On the strength of this promise, he hoped the banker would settle the demands of his most restless creditors, besides forwarding an order for £10 to the Shakespeare Hotel, Covent Garden.

The Committee met and deliberated on May 12th. They did not award him an annuity, nor did they appoint him head of a Department; but they did vote him a further cash grant of £2,000, and recommended that he be allowed to perfect his line and mortar system. Two thousand pounds was not very much, and pitifully short of Manby's enormous hopes, but it was better than nothing, and did at least serve to keep the duns at bay for a time.

The physical and mental stress of the past years had been very great. Will power, supported by hope, had kept him going. But now signs of strain were beginning to show. The injuries to his head became inflamed, he suffered from blinding headaches and spells of dizziness that made him stagger like a drunkard. On the verge of a total collapse he went back to Yarmouth and took to his bed.

His illness did not interrupt the flow of his demands upon his dearest friend. Dawson Turner was in London on a visit, and Manby, from his sick-bed, bombarded him with commissions. Would he call on Whittaker, and settle about the book, and while in the vicinity of Ludgate Hill, arrange with Bluger, the optician, who had been making modifications to the extinguisher, to pack the apparatus carefully and send it to Yarmouth? There was also Doctor Martin of the Humane Society to visit, to enquire about the award of a prize for life-saving that Manby had applied for. Then perhaps Dawson Turner would look in at the Foreign Office to find out if the Dutch and Swedish ambassadors had been informed of the forty-nine Dutch and thirteen Swedish sailors who had been saved by Manby's equipment.

It was during this period of suffering and enforced inactivity that Manby conceived the idea of founding a society devoted to the saving of life from shipwreck. He would have preferred a Government Department, but since any hope of this was now remote, he planned a private organisation, supported by subscriptions from the public, which would be capable of taking over from the Customs the control and operation of his rescue stations. He succeeded in interesting a number of influential men in the project, including the Archbishop of Canterbury and Sir William Hillary. In February 1824, when he had recovered sufficiently to return to London, a meeting was held at the City of London Tavern, and the Royal Society for the Preservation of Life from Shipwreck came into being.

Some years later, the Society changed its name to the Royal National Lifeboat Institution, and today there are few organisations more valuable or held in higher esteem. Inevitably, perhaps, it is not Manby, but Sir William Hillary[15] who is honoured as the founder.

The first official act of the new Society was to award five gold medals—to the King, the Duke of York, the Archbishop of Canterbury, Sir William Hillary—and Manby. In a more practical vein, the Society did succeed in wresting from the Customs a share in the control of Manby's apparatus. But neither the pious hopes of Parliament, nor the good intentions of the Society, made up for lack of sufficient funds. The actual number of stations set up around the coasts of the British Isles never exceeded one hundred; but at least Manby could no longer be entirely excluded, and he was able to ensure that those which did exist were efficiently operated and maintained.

To Manby, an important function of the Society was to provide him with a platform. He gave numerous lectures, sponsored by the Society, and they proved as popular in London as they had once done on the east coast. 'The object of the prevention of Shipwreck is so important,' he told Dawson Turner, 'and the methods suggested by me so clear and convincing, that I never saw such interest taken on any subject.'

He courted publicity as ardently as any actor, interspersing his lectures with outrageous asides, which made him many enemies, but delighted his audiences. He was fast becoming a celebrity, and when he went back to Yarmouth, the barracks and Sophia, as he was periodically obliged to do, life seemed very dull.

August doors, hitherto closed, and shortly to close again, opened briefly to Manby. Resplendent with his medals, he was a familiar figure in high society. He was a slightly ludicrous lion, but nevertheless a lion. Although he had courted fame, and this was fame of a sort, he knew that it was the transient, unreliable renown that any public entertainer might enjoy for a short time. Manby wanted something more; he longed for an appointment, a title and, above all, the gracious notice of Royalty. But Royalty continued to remain coldly aloof. Apart from the Duke of Kent's remark in Hyde Park, the Royal family had given no indication that they recognised his existence. Since the disastrous 'delicate investigation', Manby was a name which was it unwise to utter in the King's presence.

But there were other Royal families whose minds were not poisoned with prejudice, and it was across the Channel that prospects of a dazzling brightness suddenly opened. In the spring of 1827, a letter arrived addressed from the Palais Bourbon, and signed by the Prince de Condé, inviting Manby to visit France.

5

WITH THE REINSTATEMENT of the monarchy in France, the Bourbons had come back to their riches, their palaces and their vast estates, and had resumed their old pursuits as though the Revolution had never taken place and Napoleon had never been born.

The Prince de Condé, at St Leu or Chantilly, could now indulge to the full his partiality for women and his passion for hunting. Although he was seventy-two, his vigour and virility seemed to be inexhaustible, but his hobbies left him little time or energy for anything else. There could hardly have been a more unlikely person to show an interest in Manby or his work. The Prince's invitation was certainly remarkable, but the train of events which led to its being written was even more bizarre. It went back half a century to the Isle of Wight, and a fisherman called Dawes who had drunk himself and his large family into the Newport workhouse. One of his daughters, Sophia, an exceptionally precocious girl of fourteen, escaped and made her way to London

61

where she joined the army of child prostitutes who hawked their bodies for a few pennies in the streets and parks. It was the age of Fanny Hill, but the reality was far from a jolly romp, and few survived to write their memoirs. They died, while still in their teens, of disease or starvation.

Sophia Dawes was an exception. She bought books instead of gin, and acquired an education that qualified her for employment in a fashionable brothel. Here, between entertaining rich debauchees, she continued her studies. She was beautiful and clever; shrewd and ambitious.

The Prince, at that time the Duke de Bourbon, during his exile in London, was a regular customer of the brothel in Piccadilly. He became infatuated with Sophia, and before long had established her as his mistress in an elegant house in Gloucester Place. After the Revolution, he decided to take Sophia back to France with him. In order to preserve an appearance of respectability, he arranged for her to marry an impoverished aristocrat, the Count de Feuchères. The trusting Count was informed confidentially that his young bride was the Duke's natural daughter, and he was gratified to be given a post on the Duke's staff, even though it involved long and frequent absences from home.

Sophia Dawes, now the Barronne de Feuchères, filled the role of a great lady as though she had been born to it. She was a past-mistress of intrigue; when the Orleans family replaced the Bourbons on the throne, she contrived to stay in favour, and even when her husband discovered the truth of her relationship with the Duke, she weathered the storm.

It was the Barronne's policy to consolidate her position in French society by infiltrating as many of her relations as possible into positions of influence. She had married a niece into the Talleyrand family, and she had induced the ageing Prince to appoint her nephew, Jack Dawes, as his personal aide. The Prince treated his mistress's nephew as a son; he had already given the young man a house in Paris and an estate in the south;

soon he was to obtain for him the title of the Count de Flassons.

Jack Dawes, whose aunt had been a London prostitute, married Manby's niece, the elder of Admiral Thomas Manby's two daughters. On a visit to London, Dawes attended one of his uncle-in-law's lectures and became fired with an ambition to see Manby's apparatus established on the dangerous coast of his adopted country. No doubt there were other, less admirable motives, for the Dawes family always had one eye firmly fixed on the main chance. It is possible his real interest lay in the military applications of Manby's gunnery inventions, but in any event he became one of his most fervent and active champions. He persuaded the French Ministry of Marine to translate and publish Manby's essay on 'The Saving of Life from Shipwreck'; he hoped to arrange for Manby to present a copy to the King, which was one of the reasons why, in concert with his aunt, he had persuaded the Prince to invite Manby to stay at St Leu.

Manby, who had already been enormously thrilled at the prospect of being the uncle of a Countess, was now ecstatic. The invitation, which he regarded as one of the most flattering events of his life, proved to be irresistible. In July he wrote to Dawson Turner that he had decided to accept, and asked his friend to prepare a statement to send to all the Norwich papers, detailing 'the objects of that flattering invitation that takes me across the Channel—to show that although I am slighted by my own country, a great nation is willing to show me the attention withheld by my own country'.

He was hurt and disappointed at Dawson Turner's sour reception of the great news. The banker's attitudes and his morality were middle-class and unbending. Combined with a conventionally low opinion of the French generally, was his firm conviction that the Prince was a foolish and debauched old man, who had allowed himself to become the creature of a loose woman and her mountebank nephew. He warned Manby that he was being duped, and could only bring himself into disrepute by associating with such people. By comparison, Manby's outlook had a touching, almost childlike innocence. He accepted people as he found them, and judged them by the way they treated him. The fact that the Barronne had reached her present eminence by way of the streets and a brothel, seemed to him to be to her credit, rather than the reverse, and to demonstrate her remarkable abilities. He refused to be cowed by Dawson Turner's displeasure. He had met the Barronne, he said, and had found her, without exception, the most pleasing, accomplished and delightful woman he had ever known.

For the moment, Manby was financially independent; he did not need Dawson Turner's permission or assistance to go to France. He ignored his friend's admonitions, and wrote gaily that he had just got his passport. The Ambassador had told him that his luggage would have no unnecessary search, and the Consul General had sent him the most flattering letter he had ever read. 'He has told the Minister of Marine that I am an ornament to mankind. What a different feeling from my own narrow-minded countrymen.'

On the eve of his departure, Manby hurt his knee, and his leg was tightly swathed in bandages when he limped aboard the steam packet at Brighton. Ten hours later, after a beautiful passage, he was in Dieppe. Almost the first thing he saw was a banner flying from a house on the pier, inscribed in English: 'Strangers are in-treated to assist in finding winding sheets and coffins for unfortunate drowned persons whatever nation they may be.' Manby assisted to the tune of five francs, 'much,' he said, 'to the gratification of the members of the Society devoted to this work'.

The coach journey by way of Rouen occupied two days, and Manby reached Paris on Saturday evening. It had been arranged that Jack Dawes would meet him there, but a message at his hotel regretted that Mr Dawes was obliged to attend the Duke on a hunting trip. However, the Barronne de Feuchères would ac-

A BEAR ATTACKING A BOAT.

London Pub^d by G. & W.B.Whittaker, Ave Maria Lane

Manby about to shoot a polar bear: illustration from his
Journal of a Voyage to Greenland

The mortar used by Manby for his first experiments

Modern line-carrying rocket apparatus

company Manby to St Leu, to arrive on Wednesday evening, when the hunting was scheduled to finish and a grand dinner party was to take place. Among the guests would be the Duke of Orleans, who had expressed an anxious wish to meet Manby.

At this time Paris was crowded with English tourists, and while he awaited the Barronne, Manby joined the sightseers' circuit— the Champs-Elysées, the Louvre and Versailles. The fountains of the Great Water at Versailles quite unmanned him. 'Every jet was in fullest action,' he wrote to Dawson Turner. 'The effect was too great for me, and I was obliged to retire to conceal my feelings.' He recovered in time to see the King—all smiles and good humour—review the Swiss Guards. 'It was a day of all others for me,' he wrote, 'of the most exquisite gratification.'

There were even greater days to come, starting with the spectacular arrival at his hotel of the Barronne and her entourage of three carriages.

The Barronne, an expert at inflating male egos, completely captivated Manby. He wrote ecstatically to Dawson Turner: 'The amiable woman's anxiety about me is great indeed, to advance me in honour and fame, and she urged me, on the day I dine with the Prince, to wear my medals. How different are all these circumstances to the cold, spiteful feelings of my own countrymen—and particularly the grovelling and narrow minds of many of those who so unkindly treat me.'

To this letter, several pages in length, he added a postscript: 'Please tell my wife I am well, and daily get strength in knee.'

There were elaborate formalities to be observed by visitors to the Château St Leu, starting with a presentation to the Prince by the First Gentleman of Honour. The length of time a new arrival was left to wait in the Presence Room was, Manby had been told, an indication of his importance. The more distinguished the visitor, the quicker the Prince appeared. Manby was careful to note, and to tell Dawson Turner, that in his case only a few minutes elapsed before the Prince came into the room. 'He was most unaffected and polished,' Manby wrote, 'and for a man of seventy-two, astonishingly active and well-preserved. He had set out hunting that morning at 4 o'clock with my nephew, and had been hunting all day, but he showed no signs of fatigue. He shook me by the hand and expressed the greatest pleasure in seeing me, and gave directions for appartments to be allotted me, for use as long as I desired.'

That evening the dinner in honour of the Duke of Orleans took place. The state apartments were opened for the occasion, and the covers removed from chairs and sofas, made, it seemed to Manby, of burnished gold. Dinner was served in the great entrance hall. The flowers, the women flashing with jewellery, the servants in their gorgeous livery, were splendid indeed, but nothing could rival the clinking glitter of Manby, loaded with his medals.

Before dinner, the Prince personally introduced Manby to his brother, the future King of France. 'He paid me great attention,' Manby recorded, 'and expressed (in English) his pleasure at being introduced to a person whose name was known to all the world for his humanity and benevolence to mankind.' Prudently, Manby had in his pocket a copy of his essays on the prevention of shipwreck and destructive fires. He presented these to the Duke of Orleans who promised to study them with great care.

Manby could not speak French, and made no attempt to do so. When, the following week, he visited the Ministry of Marine, Jack Dawes went with him to act as interpreter. The Minister had disappointing news; the King was away at St Cloud, and it had not been possible to arrange the expected audience. The Frenchman softened the blow with effusive Gallic tact. 'He told me,' Manby wrote to Dawson Turner, 'that he was sure his Sovereign would take the same delight as himself in being known to a man so distinguished for his humanity and good acts. He pressed me to return in November when he was sure the King would receive me and show me that attention to which my merit entitled me from every nation.'

In the evening, the Barronne invited him to join her party at the Théâtre Français in a box lent her by Prince Talleyrand. During the performance the legendary Prince himself looked in to be introduced to Manby. It was a splendid climax to a splendid visit. Never had Manby been treated with such deference and respect; never had he hobnobbed on such familiar terms with the noble and the Royal. Although, in practical terms, his visit had achieved very little, it had nevertheless been more than worth while. The foundations had been laid for prospects of unimaginable brightness.

The deference and attention persisted all the way home to Dover. At Calais he dined with the British Consul, whose 'kindness and eagerness to assist, was precisely what had occurred in France whenever my name had been announced'. His name seemed suddenly to have taken on a magic quality; even the sight of it on his trunks he said, excited eager attention, while at Dover, the Collector of Customs' behaviour was peculiarly pleasing.

From Dover, he wrote to Dawson Turner that his visit to France had been the proudest moment of his life, and he was convinced that 'if Providence spares me for a few more years, I shall be most distinguishedly placed, not only in high honour, but in the enjoyment of profitable situations—the best reproach for the very ungenerous conduct I have received from my native country'.

The letter concluded with grandiose directions for his homecoming. He was undecided whether to travel by coach or coastal steamer, so it would be necessary for a servant with a barrow for his luggage to be stationed at the Bear Inn, as well as a boat standing ready at the jetty house, in case he should come by sea. As an afterthought, he added a postscript: 'Please tell my wife.'

Manby's first visit to France had been a success; his second was to be a triumph. In October, his translated essay, dedicated to

King Charles the Tenth, was published, and the same month he received a letter from the Prince expressing his anxiety to see Manby again, and inviting him to Chantilly to take part in the festivities in honour of St Hubert, the patron saint of the chase.

To be courted in this way was the realisation of Manby's most persistent dream. He did not ask why the French had taken him to their hearts with such abandon. It would have been an ungrateful question, and a difficult one to answer. It was sufficient for Manby that the rulers of France, whatever their motives, treated him in a manner usually reserved for great noblemen, ambassadors and intimate friends.

At the beginning of November, Manby packed his medals and his fanciest waistcoats and set out for Chantilly. He tried to persuade Dawson Turner to go with him. The banker, after all, spoke French, and would be so useful as an interpreter; and think how splendid it would be to be able to take his friend to the First Gentleman, the Marquis de Villequantes, to be introduced to his other friend, the Prince de Condé. But Dawson Turner, still grimly disapproving, declined. Manby consoled himself with the thought that with Dawson Turner in Yarmouth there would at least be someone to look after Sophia.

Chantilly, although extensively damaged in the Revolution, was vastly more magnificent than St Leu. As for the company, 'The number of nobles that are here,' Manby wrote breathlessly, 'Princes, Dukes, Marquesses and titled characters, is almost incredible.' Better still, there were numerous beautiful and elegant women, including the Barronne de Feuchères, 'who gives me,' Manby wrote, 'what I most desire—approbation.'

The Festival of St Hubert turned out to be a stag slaughtering orgy on a fantastic scale. Manby sent Dawson Turner a detailed account in daily instalments with instructions to correct the French words which he had written as pronounced, and then to forward it to the *Norwich Mercury*.

Early on the morning of the first day, a splendid cavalcade of state carriages, the horses richly caparisoned, arrived to take the Prince and his guests to breakfast in the forest. The Prince sent a message that he particularly wished Captain Manby to sit with him in the leading coach. So, with the little Barrack Master of Yarmouth taking precedence, the nobility of France set off along the glorious autumnal avenues until they reached a clearing where a large tent had been pitched. 'Here,' wrote Manby, 'a sumptuous repast awaited, with every delicacy to please the eye or gratify the palate, including the head of an immense wild boar. Smaller booths, stored with provisions, had also been erected to supply the wants of a crowd of some thousand persons who had gathered to await the Prince's arrival.'

While the company feasted, the retinue of the chase took up stations in the avenues. There were the *valets de chien* with the hounds, the huntsman and his army of *picqueurs* and fifty mounted grooms leading horses for the *chasseurs* and visitors. They all wore the gaudy livery of the Bourbons—scarlet jackets, trimmed with silver, and laced cocked hats.

Shortly after breakfast, the huntsman reported that a stag had been located. Amid cheers from the crowd, the Prince and his party mounted—Manby was provided with a well behaved hack —and, with the crowd following on foot, the unequal contest began. The deer bounded across a glade with the hounds in pursuit. 'The stillness of the day,' wrote Manby, 'reverberated with the grand chorus of hounds, and the animating tones of the horns.' Nothing was now wanting, he felt, but a good vocalist to sing the British hunting song, 'This day a stag must die'.

The chase lasted two hours, and when at last the hounds caught the exhausted stag, it was shot to prevent injury. The whole party then returned to the tent, 'to which place,' said Manby, 'the victim of our pursuit was brought on the shoulders of the populace'. The wretched carcase was laid in front of the tent and an ancient and extremely gruesome ceremony performed. The huntsman cut off the deer's forefoot, handed it to the Master of

Horse, who in turn handed it to the Prince. The animal was then 'disrobed of its skin', while the ravenous hounds were kept at bay with whips. Then everyone who had a horn raised it to his lips and sounded 'the death of the stag'. Finally, 'the pack of hounds, chanting to their fullest strain the melody of the chase, were, on a given signal, allowed to rush in and devour their well-earned prize'.

That night a banquet, 'confirming the House of Condé having the best cooks, wines and fruits in France', was held in the celebrated stables of Chantilly. Two hundred guests, the men loaded with decorations, the women flashing with diamonds, sat down at a crescent table beneath the great central dome. The gallery surrounding the dome was packed with members of the public who had been graciously allowed in to witness the splendid scene.

After dinner, a screen surrounding the table 'disappeared as if by magic, revealing an elegantly fitted-up theatre, formed by the West wing of the stables. The pit was filled with well-dressed persons from the neighbourhood, while there was a box in front of the stage for the Prince and his party.' Between the acts of a play performed by some gifted amateurs, wine in all varieties was served in the box, refreshments were taken to the pit and even the public in the rotunda was given free punch.

The following day, hunting was resumed with a variation known as a *battue*. The object was simply to slaughter as many animals as possible, each hunter being allowed to keep his bag. An army of beaters, working in crescent formation, cornered a large number of animals for the guests to shoot. Manby noted some unsportsmanlike behaviour, and regarded it as a miracle that besides masses of beasts, a number of beaters were not killed.

Dinner that night was in the Grand Gallery, with music and dancing into the small hours. At nine o'clock, the indefatigable Prince was ready in his carriage to convey a few specially selected guests back to the forest. Manby was among the chosen, and once again had the honour of sitting next to the Prince. They breakfasted at a romantic castle, deep in the forest, backed by mountains and fronted by an extensive lake. After breakfast, they pursued a stag up, down and around the mountain, until in desperation it plunged into the lake. The professional huntsmen took to boats, while carriages arrived at the shore, loaded with beautiful women to see the kill. 'The effect,' said Manby, 'was one of inexpressible delight.'

Manby's solicitude towards mankind seemed to be matched by a callous indifference to the suffering of lower animals. Provided it was all done in the name of sport, and indulged in by Royal personages and beautiful ladies, he experienced inexpressible delight at the most dreadful and senseless cruelty. But there were limits. As he watched the huntsmen in their boats closing in on the floundering stag, he felt suddenly sickened and ashamed. 'My feelings towards the deer became changed,' he wrote, 'when I heard its piteous moans on the boats approaching him, probably aware of his fate—but when I saw the gallant stag that had afforded me so much gratification in the pursuit, despatched by a knife driven into his head, I must admit it strangely excited my compassion.'

The stag, leaving a trail of blood across the lake, to the further delight of the ladies in their carriages, was towed ashore, and the barbaric dismembering ceremonies performed. Then the Master of Horns sounded the Retreat, and the party returned to Chantilly, ready to partake of a sumptuous repast and to finish the day with dancing.

It was the end of a glorious week for Manby, if not for the stags. The extraordinary partiality which the Prince had shown him was amply reciprocated. The Prince, he declared, was an honour to France and an ornament to the world. Greater glories were to follow. Word came from Paris that arrangements had been made for him to be presented to the King, and afterwards, to the Dauphin. The date chosen, by a happy coincidence, was November 28th—his sixty-third birthday. Manby's elation was unbounded. In a royal carriage put at his disposal by the Prince, he dashed to Paris to prepare himself for the great moment. Only one thing marred his happiness; once again he was desperately short of money.

The little that had remained of his £2,000 after staving off his most pressing creditors, had been swallowed up by the expenses of his French jaunts. Now he owed money on both sides of the Channel. There was £150 outstanding for translating and printing his essay, and there would be the additional cost of special binding for the copies he intended to present to the King and the Dauphin. There would also be the expense of providing himself with suitable clothes. In a country where even the dogs' valets were decked in lace and silver brocade, something elaborate was clearly required when he appeared before the King.

'This will necessarily put me to some expense,' he wrote to Dawson Turner, 'but is not the object too important to let a few pounds prevent?'

The banker must have sighed, for it was only too plain who would have to pay for Manby's finery. He did pay, but with a marked lack of enthusiasm. It was not Dawson Turner alone who disapproved of Manby's infatuation with the French. The extra-ordinary patience of his employers, the Barrack Board, was beginning to show signs of strain. It was, after all, scarcely reasonable to expect them to grant Manby indefinite leave of absence, and to pay him his Barrack Master's salary, simply to benefit a nation that had only recently ceased to be England's bitterest enemy. But even if he lost his job; even if he had to appear in rags, nothing would have kept Manby from his appointment on November 28th.

6

FOR WHAT HAPPENED when Manby, in his hired silk breeches and his medals, met the King of France, there is only his own account, written immediately afterwards and sent to Dawson Turner. Dawson Turner viewed it with suspicion, although he had not yet reached the point of accusing his friend of downright lying. This was to come later, when he was asked to believe what seemed to him totally incredible—Manby's description of his interview with Princess Victoria. As far as his meeting with Charles the Tenth was concerned, it was not the facts that were so difficult to accept, as the general tone of the detail.

'On the occasion of being presented to the King,' Manby wrote, 'and in the presence of such a numerous and splendid suite, you would naturally have expected that I should be awestruck. No; quite the reverse, for on the monarch seeing me, a most affable smile beaming on his countenance, he condescended to address me immediately in good English: "I am glad to see you." This gave me self-possession, and I could not resist, on presenting the book—probably to deviate from the correct line of etiquette—to say: "Accept, I most humbly beseech Your Majesty, the warmest tribute of an Englishman's gratitude, for the noble interest you have taken in the cause of humanity, particularly that of saving a class of man so important to a maritime nation, for which may God Almighty bless you with a long and happy life."

'Whether it was from the energetic manner of expressing my sincerity, I know not; but with a smile that looked as if it came from the heart, he said: "I kindly thank you." He then assured me he would read my publication with lively interest. In my interview I scrupulously avoided the slightest appearance of self-interest, and showed my desire to be, what it really is, to benefit mankind, not myself. I may be blamed by some for such feelings, but a noble heart never will.'[1]

He saw the King in the morning; in the afternoon he was at the Tuileries for a session with the Dauphin, Grand Admiral of France. The Dauphin expressed great interest in Manby's shore-to-ship rescue system, and told him that it had already been decided to install the apparatus at the Port of Brest.

'I am known in Paris as the most indefatigable man possible,' Manby wrote, 'I have done wonders in a few days. Since my interview with the King, many distinguished men not only view my plan in a more favourable light, but are exerting themselves to extend the system to all dangerous shores of France.'[2]

Even the British Ambassador, it seemed, was hurriedly climbing on the band-waggon. 'The world,' Lord Granville told Manby, 'appreciates your labours.' Lady Granville sent him an invitation to a splendid soirée; but Manby was now in the delightful position of being able to play hard to get. Although he had withstood the rigours of wining, dining and dancing at St Leu and Chantilly, he now 'feared the effects that invariably attend very hot rooms', and declined the invitation.[3]

It was all most gratifying. Only one incident cast a tiny shadow across the brilliance of Manby's triumph. Sir Thomas Gooch, his brother-in-law, was in Paris at the time and by chance the two men met in the street. 'When I accosted him in a friendly manner,' Manby described the encounter, 'he did not reply, but turned and walked away. Whether this proceeded from pride or ignorance, I know not.'4

Manby had hoped, while in Paris, to see the Minister of the Interior and the Prefect General, to put before them his plans for the prevention of destructive fires. But at the beginning of December there was a General Election, and not only were the Ministers fully occupied, but there was a good deal of uncertainty how long they would remain in office. Manby's leave, and his money, in any event, had both run out. It was time to return to reality. The prospect was uninviting, and before he went he could not resist going back to Chantilly for a few more days in fairyland.

'As a lover of my native land,' he wrote, 'I really regret the character of England, the coldness, nay the unkindness, I have received from several in the highest departments of life, and the unwillingness of many others to allow me any—nay, the desire to pluck from me—the credit that may be my due. This has often given me a heartfelt pang. But the noble and generous attention of all towards me in this country does them the highest honour, and chases from my mind what has given me so much pain, particularly in that County in which I drew my first breath.'5

Before he finally left for home, Manby was presented with yet another medal—a magnificent specimen in solid gold—in recognition of his distinguished services to France.

However welcome he might be at the court of Charles the Tenth of France, Manby's chances of favourable notice by the King of England were non-existent so long as George the Fourth occupied the throne. Although it was not Manby's fault that his brother had refused to admit having been the Queen's lover, he had played a part in thwarting the King's scheme to rid himself of an uncongenial and inconvenient wife. If Manby's account of what occurred were true, there is little doubt the King would have heard about it.

At the time of the 'Delicate Investigation' the two Manby brothers were staying together at a London coffee-house. One evening, Colonel MacMahon, the Prince's sleazy private secretary, called, and left a letter for Thomas Manby. It contained what was, in effect, a blank cheque, which Thomas was invited to fill in for any amount he chose up to £40,000, provided he would give evidence against the Princess. Manby's reaction when he was shown this letter, was an excess of righteous indignation.

'You ought to have seized the disreputable pander by the collar,' he exclaimed, 'and never let him out of your grasp until he had given up the name of the person who dared to make so ignoble and dishonourable a proposal, and exposed him to infamy.'[6]

These sentiments, however admirable they might have seemed at the time, did not dispose the Prince, when he became King, to lavish honours upon the man who had uttered them.

But now the King seemed about to pay the penalty for a lifetime of excess, and it was unlikely that his grotesque bulk would weigh down the throne very much longer, Manby's hopes of royal favour revived. The heir apparent was the Duke of Clarence, Lord High Admiral, a man, Manby felt, who could hardly be indifferent to the great work of saving sailors' lives. Before leaving for France, Manby had sent the Duke a copy of his essay. This had never been acknowledged, and Manby told Dawson Turner that he doubted if the Lord High Admiral had been allowed to see it. It was Manby's determination, immediately he arrived back in England, to seek a personal interview with the Duke to discover 'whether the work I had the honour of dedicating to him is worthy of the notice of an English Prince'.

This plan was frustrated by the Barrack Board who, as soon as he set foot on English soil, ordered him peremptorily to return to Yarmouth and his duties at the barracks.

After the glamour of his French adventure, after having been so long at the hub of things in London, life at Yarmouth seemed very bleak. He was like a resting actor, pining for the limelight, the applause, the hope of miraculous recognition and fame overnight. Even affluent domesticity would have bored him; as it was, impoverished, daily involved in disputes with tradesmen over unpaid bills, it was unbearable. His military duties offered little relief. These, too, were petty and mainly concerned with minor crimes and childish quarrels. He did his best to settle down; and in his way, he *was* a devoted husband. But he and Sophia were beings from different worlds—she gentle, frail, uncomprehending and immobile; he restless, fanatical, self-centred and plagued with desires she could not understand.

He stuck it out for six months, occupying his time perfecting his invention of a gunlock for firing by percussion, the oblong shell which exploded on impact, and a device for firing two shots simultaneously. In June he was back in London, this time with the blessing of the Board, who had ordered him to submit his inventions for expert examination at Woolwich.

The colonel commanding was impressed. 'He said,' Manby recorded, 'that there was a strong prejudice against the means of exploding by percussion but that I had removed in a most ingenious way certain parts from which the prejudice arose. He told me the lock was the most ingenious thing of the kind ever brought to his examination, and the oblong shell the most destructive missile he had ever seen.' Manby also took his plans and models to the Admiralty. 'Lord Manvers said my inventive mind knew no bounds,' he wrote to Dawson Turner, 'equally great in the preservation and destruction of life.' Manby was promised that full-scale tests would be made by the Navy, but nearly four years were to elapse before they took place.

Later the same week, the Annual General Meeting of the Royal National Institute was held at the City of London Tavern. The

Institute's main achievement during the year had been the saving of thirty-four lives by means of Manby's apparatus. Apart from this, there were only lectures, dinners and the issue of medals to report. One of the sharpest chips on Manby's shoulder was the way in which Sir William Hillary had usurped him as Founder of the Institute, and he noted with grim satisfaction that the toast to Hillary was greeted with half-hearted and embarrassed applause, while the following one to himself was received with unbounded enthusiasm. Crumbs such as these were a poor substitute for the solid diet of official recognition he craved; but they were all Manby had to sustain him and he devoured them ravenously.

In August Manby, always accident prone, fell down some steps and broke his leg. He was obliged to return to Yarmouth, where Sophia and her companion, Frost, became his nurses and his hand-maidens. Immobilised and depressed, he decided it was time to select his biographer. The honour fell to Dawson Turner, to whom he sent a great mass of papers, including a detailed account of the attempt on his life by Captain Pogson. He gave strict instructions, however, that the 'mysterious as well as suspicious' circumstances were not to be revealed until after his death. He also sent four of the pellets that had been taken out of his head, together with an unfired pellet for comparison, 'as it may be interesting, as well as useful, to the examiner of my head after I am no more, to show what the head is able to undergo, and to point out the advantages to owners of thick skulls'.[7]

When his leg had healed, he suffered from an inflammation of the eyes which nearly blinded him, but did not prevent him from becoming involved in an unsavoury quarrel with a man called Yeth. Manby considered Yeth had in some way insulted him and, as he told Dawson Turner, 'I never did, nor never could, brook an insult without procuring satisfaction, either when I am opposed to a gentleman, or one who I ought to have treated with the greatest contempt.'

Manby's method of procuring satisfaction was to insult Yeth back—harder. He spread the tale that Yeth, a married man, was having an affair with another woman. The dispute caused a great stir among the gentry of Norfolk. Sir Thomas Gooch took full advantage of the opportunity to intensify his anti-Manby campaign, claiming that Manby's behaviour proved what he had always maintained, that Manby was a blackguard.

Yeth, not being a gentleman, instead of calling Manby out, put the matter in the hands of his lawyer. The prospect of having to pay damages in a slander action was much more serious for Manby than that of fighting a duel, especially as Dawson Turner refused to take his side. Faced with the very real possibility of the dispute ending, for him, in a debtors' prison, Manby climbed down, and wrote a humiliating letter of apology.

But there were other letters, more pleasant, and certainly more hopeful. A letter he had written to Peel, more or less as a matter of routine, requesting that his essay on shipwreck be presented to the King, had resulted in a most promising reply from the great man's private secretary. This was remarkable considering that all his previous letters to Peel had been ignored. As soon as he was well enough, Manby travelled back to London for an interview with the secretary, who continued to be recklessly encouraging. Whether it was all a joke, or the result of a misunderstanding, he convinced Manby that Peel was arranging for him to present his essay to the King in person. He clothed his farce in circumstantial detail, asking to see the medals Manby would be wearing, and advising him that he must be prepared to answer the King's questions about them— particularly the French one, which, he said 'will now be most interesting as well as of great historical importance'. It all seemed so real, Manby laid out three guineas on the hire of a Court outfit. He even went so far as to leave a card at the Lord Chamberlain's office ready for the great occasion: 'Captain G. W. Manby, presented by Sir Robert Peel, Bart. to deliver to the King a treatise on the preservation of Mariners from stranded vessels and the prevention of shipwreck; with a statement of the number of subjects saved of different nations by the plans introduced by him.'[8]

The King, in fact, was dying, and there was no possibility of his seeing anyone, least of all Manby. While Manby waited for the summons that was never to come, he lavished his own patronage on the elder of the brothers Joy, whom he had brought with him from Yarmouth. He took the young man to stay with Admiral Cunningham at the Chatham dockyards to discuss details of a marine painting the Admiral had commissioned. Manby was delighted to observe the coachman's son acquit himself so well in company, especially, he told Dawson Turner, 'among elegant and accomplished females'. At dinner, Joy amused the ladies by sketching 'a large foreign dog who has his meals when they have theirs, and enjoys himself on the rug'.

Sir Thomas Gooch, since he had become head of the family, had done everything in his power to cut Manby and his wife off from any contact with her relations. This was distressing to the kind and gentle Sophia and, in particular, she felt very deeply her exclusion from helping, or even seeing, her sister Elizabeth, who was dying of cancer. Elizabeth's disease was extremely unpleasant, and the baronet had exiled her to miserable lodgings at Edmonton under the care of an old woman. Sophia was prepared to take Elizabeth into her own house, where she could at least die in comfort, but Sir Thomas refused to allow the move. His motive was straightforward, and he was prepared to tell it to anyone. Elizabeth had a little money of her own, and he was determined Manby should not get his hands on it.

While he was in London Manby called repeatedly at Sir Thomas's town house, and was at last granted a curt interview. Manby's pleas failed to move his brother-in-law; but he did agree to drive Manby over to Edmonton to see Elizabeth. However, when the time arrived, he sent a servant with the message that he

It seemed to me, even when the ice was broken to a great extent, that the ladders might be used with still more effect by means of a buoyant wicker-boat, covered with canvass, in the manner shown in the cut, which exhibits the but end of the ladder resting on the ice, while

Wicker-Boat and Ladder.

the other lies on the boat, which is thus kept steady, while it affords a larger area than the ladder, used by itself, to the men who are endeavouring to extricate the unfortunate person, and admits of more disengaged efforts,

Ladders are also readily furnished with a floating platform, by a small cask (those in which tamarinds are imported are well adapted

A page from Manby's 'Essay on the Means of Saving Persons from Drowning'

61

Finding a chest inconvenient, I conveyed the above apparatus in a
cart, so light that a person can wheel it with rapidity to the required

spot. The vessels, too, combine the means of projecting the fluid
with force at pleasure; are portable, and, when slung across the
shoulders, may be carried up a ladder, or to any part of the building
on fire, however difficult of access. The design of this apparatus,
charged as above with the Antiphlogistic Fluid, was to keep up a
constant play, so as, if early applied, to subdue the fire, or, at least,
check its progress, until the arrival of the regular engines.

A page from Manby's 'Essay on the Extinction and Prevention
of Destructive Fires'

'declined going', adding that if Manby cared to walk to the City, he could take the stage. Although it was pouring with rain, Manby set out on foot. He missed the stage, but managed to get a lift in a butcher's cart.

'Scarcely ever in my life,' he told Dawson Turner, 'did I meet with a man of such startling good sense, and the journey passed with satisfaction. On my arrival at Edmonton, I was shown to the wretched apartment of my sister-in-law. I stated the anxious wish of my wife to afford her asylum under my roof. She looked astonished, as she had been led to believe that Mrs Manby was the cause of her being sent away, and her other sister was the kind and attentive one. I, however, placed it in the opposite view, without saying anything to her distress. Asking her what I could get for her, she said "a little money". I said her sister had given me a crown piece to lay out for her. She appeared most grateful.' He had also brought for her as a present a small glass harmonica, and as he left, he heard her picking out the notes of God Save the King.[9] A week later she was dead.

The King also died that week, and Manby's hopes, if he had nourished any, of a legacy from his sister-in-law, as well as those of an audience with George the Fourth, vanished together. For the time being, the Court dress was returned to its owner, and Manby hurriedly mounted a campaign to bring himself to the attention of William the Fourth. There was no time to be lost, for all sorts of persons would doubtless be pressing their claims for favour upon the new monarch.

The Sailor King was at Brighton, mourning his brother in his brother's rococo pavilion. By a fortunate coincidence, Manby's brother, the Admiral, happened to be living at Brighton at the time, so there was a ready-made headquarters in Marine Square at which Manby arrived on October 12th. He left his name at the Pavilion, together with a personal note to the King's secretary, Sir Herbert Taylor,[10] requesting an interview. To his delight,

Taylor replied immediately, inviting him to attend at two o'clock the following day.

When Manby arrived at the Pavilion, he was astonished to find that instead of the confidential chat he had expected, he was shown into a room packed with fashionably dressed and argumentative women. It seemed that Taylor was in the process of sorting out the late King's scandalous entanglements, and Manby had been included by a clerical error.[11]

Manby decided that the most effective way to attract attention to himself was to give a lecture. He put an advertisement in the local paper, and wrote to Dawson Turner for his trunk of models to be sent immediately, well corded up. Tickets were half-a-crown, the proceeds to go to the Sussex County Hospital. He wrote that he hoped Dawson Turner would not disapprove of this charitable gesture, which had, in fact, already produced dividends. 'The liberality of my offer had such an effect on the proprietor of the rooms intended for the lecture, that he sent word: "Captain Manby is extremely welcome to any room he may select in my house gratuitously." '

Manby sent an invitation to the King, but the reply, through Taylor, regretted that His Majesty would be prevented from attending by pressure of public business. It did seem, however, from the number of high-ranking naval officers at the lecture, including Sir Robert Otway,[12] rumoured to be the King's particular favourite and consulted on all occasions, that the King had sent his representatives to report. This speculation became, in Manby's mind, a certainty, when after the highly successful lecture, Otway sought him out and told him that his name and his services were frequently mentioned by the King, and there was no doubt his splendid abilities would soon be recognised. He went even further, and actually suggested that he was authorised to enquire whether a knighthood would be acceptable.

Manby believed every word. 'Time, and perhaps that very

shortly,' he wrote joyously to Dawson Turner, 'will produce what you most desire I should receive.'

That he was at last truly in the full ambience of Royal favour seemed to be confirmed, when early Sunday morning an invitation to attend the Royal Chapel arrived by special messenger. After the service, strolling in the autumn sunlight along the esplanade, he again met Otway. Otway took his arm confidentially, and said that he had told the King at dinner the infinite gratification Manby's lecture had given him. The King's remarks had been most flattering. With winks and nudges, he left Manby in no doubt that the question of his knighthood had already been decided. 'Should a certain *event* take place,' Manby wrote to Dawson Turner, 'I must draw on your bank for the amount of the fees.'

When the King left Brighton for the opening of Parliament, Manby followed immediately, taking lodgings at a coffee house near Charing Cross. It might appear, he wrote, that he did not intend to return home. This was certainly not so, but there was a great deal at stake, and never a happier moment for him to attain honour, fame and rewards. He trusted to Dawson Turner to see that his wife had everything she required, and to call in a doctor should she fall ill. 'Mrs Manby,' he said, 'is totally unacquainted with accounts—the person who attends her keeps them—but she should be amply provided with money for the present.'

In reality, Mrs Manby had no money at all, and it must have been trying for Dawson Turner, who was keeping the household going out of his own pocket, to learn from daily letters how Manby himself was squandering money in London. He had paid two guineas to 'a person distinguished for literary attainment' to put into shape for publication his lecture on the prevention of destructive fires. He had also, at some expense, but to best advantage, secured a place in the narrowest part of the Strand, to see the procession when the King went to dine with the Lord Mayor. In the event, this was money thrown away. The King's visit to the City was cancelled at the last moment, for fear of mob violence.

He was disappointed about the procession, but otherwise everything was turning out beyond his highest hopes. A person belonging to the Court had mentioned honourable rank, and he had again met Sir Robert Otway who told him: 'I had a long conversation last evening with one who is in constant attendance of the King, respecting you, who advised me to tell Captain Manby that the day is close at hand when he will receive from the King the rewards to which his distinguished merit has so justly a claim.'

In a few days it would be his sixty-fifth birthday, and he could not help thinking back to what the fortune-teller had said as to the destiny of a person born on November 28th, 1765 at 6 o'clock in the evening. He had always had a strong presentiment, he told Dawson Turner, that if he lived to attain his sixty-fifth year, much of her opinion would be realised. 'If Providence spares my life,' he wrote, 'and extends it beyond next Sunday, I cannot help having a religious hope that something important to me will occur before the close of the year, from the analogy of the year of my birth and that of my age.'

Providence did spare his life until Sunday. For this delusive boon he gave thanks to God at morning service at St Paul's. Afterwards, he wandered among the tombstones and studied the commemorative plaques. 'I could not refrain,' he told Dawson Turner, 'from offering up a wish, and a determination, to devote the residue of my life to obtain the register of my name in that great National Mausoleum.'

His two young protégés, the Joy brothers, came to supper, and the three closed the day eating plum pudding, and drinking a bumper of punch. Manby went to sleep content, convinced that on his next birthday the toast would be 'Sir George William Manby'.

7

THE YEAR 1831 OPENED for Manby with great hopes and furious activity. Miraculously, the tide of his affairs seemed to have turned. He was elected an honorary Fellow of the Royal Society; there was a possibility he might get the Order of Merit,[1] and, above all, he was supremely confident that his knighthood was now only a matter of course and of waiting for the Coronation Honours List.

There was so much to do, and it was so important to be on the spot in London, that the Barrack Board could scarcely have chosen a less convenient moment to insist that he spend more time in Yarmouth. The disturbed state of the country, they claimed, made this essential. Manby was obliged to commute between London and Yarmouth, which besides being expensive, was also a great strain on his health. He suffered from rheumatism, he could not sleep and the inflammation of his eyes returned. But he could not afford to succumb; too much was at stake. At last, in July, he wrote to Dawson Turner: 'I have laid the foundations of everything to supply my future wants, and gratify my wishes, and will therefore now take care of my health.'

When the Coronation Honours were published in the autumn, Manby's name was not included. Only a few days before, Otway had told him that the business would certainly be completed to his fullest wishes, and Lord Melbourne's secretary had assured him that a knighthood was definite.

The shock and disappointment very nearly killed Manby. The props had been knocked from under him, and he collapsed. In a miserable letter to his friend, he wrote that he had not been out of the house for a week from ailings of body and mind. He had nearly lost his sight and the pains in head were excruciating.

'I will no longer conceal from you,' he wrote, 'the principal cause—the very unexpected refusal of my King to bestow upon me some mark of his gracious favour. It is a dagger to my heart, and will, I am sure, materially shorten my days, feeling as I do my having strong claims—that of saving the lives of his subjects, particularly sailors, some at great hazard of the loss of my own life. I think posterity will say a British King, bred to the Naval Profession, should not have disregarded the solicitations made.'[2]

It seemed for a time as though Manby would never recover; the dagger to his heart had struck home very deep. He stayed at Yarmouth, a broken man. His headaches grew worse, and now, besides the infection of his eyes, outbreaks of erysipelas disfigured his face. All his restless energy disappeared, and the mind that had teemed with so many hopeful plans was now obsessed with one futile, maddening and unanswerable question: Why?

On the rare occasions he left the barracks, he wandered about Yarmouth, a wasted little old man, muttering to himself, glaring vacantly, an object of derision and pity. Sophia could do nothing to help or comfort him, or restore his self-confidence. She could not understand his tragedy, because she had never shared his dreams. They lived together at the barracks, isolated from the outside world and strangers to each other.

It was not only the King's refusal of a knighthood—although this was the heaviest blow—that was driving Manby insane. The whole world seemed abruptly to have turned against him. Enemies he did not know existed came out in the open, intent on robbing him of the one thing that was left—the credit for the shore-to-ship apparatus. Bell's claim as prior inventor was re-aired, and malicious paragraphs appeared in the papers, denigrating Manby and his achievements.

Relief came from an unexpected quarter. Manby's invention of a percussion gun-lock, an oblong, explosive shell and a means of firing two shots from one gun simultaneously, had been gathering dust for years. In the summer of 1833, the Admiralty rediscovered them and decided to hold sea trials.[3] Manby's old buoyancy and optimism started to seep back; a trickle at first, but once the breach had been made, it soon became a flood. His fortune, once again, was made; great honours awaited him as the man who had ensured the supremacy of British Naval power for the next one hundred years.

He was conscious of the irony that recognition should come to him for the destruction, and not the saving of life. But this could be rationalised, and his conscience repressed, by the useful sophistry that ultimately his inventions would reduce the loss of life in warfare. In this, as in so many other things, he was ahead of his time.

The trials were arranged to take place at Portsmouth, aboard the *Excellent* commanded by Captain Hastings.[4] Manby travelled down early in September. On the road, he told Dawson Turner, he passed the young Queen of Portugal. 'I bowed to her, and was gracefully acknowledged,' he said. This seemed to him a good omen. The graceful smile of Royalty, even though it might only be Portuguese, warmed and reassured him as common smiles could not.

The following morning he was at the King's Stairs, where a

boat from the *Excellent* was waiting for him. On board, Captain Hastings welcomed him, and introduced him to the ship's officers. 'It was very flattering,' Manby wrote, 'to be recognised and acknowledged as the man to whom not only the Service, but mankind in general was so indebted.'

The trials were spread over a month. Hastings pressed Manby to stay on the ship, but Manby found 'that my mind works best and is most active when I am alone. I have provided myself with comfortable lodgings opposite the "Victory"—the ship where Nelson yielded his last breath and imperishable name. My pursuits prevent my ever obtaining such glory, but my effort shall do the utmost not to let the name of Manby sink into oblivion, and however unkindly treated I may be by the low-bred and envious, my exertions shall be to make that name respected by those whose good opinion holds any value.'[5]

He went with Hastings to visit the *Victory*, where the officers, he said, 'honoured me by having lunch ready. Afterwards I examined every part of the great, floating bulwark, and shed a tear on being shown the spot where the Hero fell, and where he breathed his last.'

The progress of the trials exceeded, he said, his highest hopes. 'My gun-lock was highly approved for its great simplicity, and the only doubt was that it wanted strength to resist the violent concussion when used on heavy guns. It was, however, admitted by all the experts to be unquestionably by far the best lock that had ever been submitted to them.' Trials of his two-shot device were held up while wooden cups to hold the shells were manufactured, but Captain Hastings stated in the presence of all his officers 'that the plan for firing two shot did me the highest credit, and was looked on by him as a most important invention'.[6]

From the deck of the *Excellent*, while Manby watched the guns in practice, his eyes strayed from the floating targets towards the green coastline of the Isle of Wight, hazily discernible across the Solent. Somewhere on that island was the Duchess of Kent, living in widowed retirement with her daughter, Victoria, and her consoling secretary, Sir James Conroy. For years Manby had treasured the words of the late Duke on the memorable day of the Hyde Park demonstration. 'I am sure,' the Duke had said, 'your country will be grateful to you.'

This, the only token of encouragement he had ever received from the Royal Family, was now assuming a new significance. Because of her legitimacy, a quality rare among George the Third's numerous grand-children, the Duke of Kent's daughter would almost certainly inherit the Throne. Then, at last, there might be a monarch, innocent of prejudice, who, like her father, would recognise and reward his merit. Perhaps his knighthood had, after all, only been delayed; and the delay might be short, for the King had been sixty-eight on his last birthday. Although this was exactly the same age as his own, Manby never doubted that he would be the one to survive.

It was possible that the young princess had been deliberately kept in ignorance of Manby's great services; or, worse, attempts could have been made to poison her mind against him. In either case, Manby decided it was imperative to visit the Isle of Wight. If he could not directly influence the daughter, he could, at least, make an advocate of her mother.

Manby chose a favourable moment, when the trials were at a standstill awaiting delivery of the two-shot apparatus. Then, armed with a letter of introduction to Conroy from the Commander-in-Chief, Portsmouth, and several copies of his essay on 'The Preservation of Life from Shipwreck', he took the early morning packet, bound for East Cowes.

As with his interview with the King of France, there is only Manby's own account[7] of what took place when he presented himself at Norris Castle, where the Royal Standard was flying to denote the Duchess was in residence. According to Manby, he was first seen by Conroy, 'to whom I stated the object of my visit, hoping he would honour me by presenting the book, and

also the letter to the Duchess of Kent'. Conroy immediately
replied: 'I shall do it with great pleasure, but first, let me assure
you that Princess Victoria well knows Captain Manby, as she
considers it part of her studies to learn and be intimately acquainted
with every character who she considers a benefactor to mankind.'

The secretary then left the room, taking the book and letter
with him. After a few minutes he returned 'with the Duchess's
best thanks, and wish to see me and make her personal acknow-
ledgement. On my being ushered into a splendid apartment, she
soon appeared, with my letter in one hand and the book in the
other. She said she would reserve giving it to her daughter until
in my presence, for her to thank me herself as soon as her morning
studies are over. She soon did appear, and I was struck by her
graceful, easy manner, and—I shall never forget—an eye of such
penetration, as I never before beheld in one so young.

'While the Duchess and I were in conversation, Victoria's eye
was earnestly fixed on me, a sweet smile playing on her countenance. I stated to the Duchess the late Duke's interest in me and my
experiments, and the encouragement he gave me and my endeav-
ours to obtain his patronage. I had, I said, the strongest reasons
to deplore his loss. The Duchess looked at Victoria, and then asked
me if I thought she were like her father. I replied, most strongly,
and that I had no doubt equally so in greatness and benevolence
of mind.

'The Duchess then presented the book, stating it was the saving
of persons from shipwreck, accompanied by a request that her
Royal daughter would read it. This request was energetically
responded to. "Yes," said Victoria, "I will not only read it, but
get it by heart." As I took my leave, I observed that the Princess
had my little volume pressed to her bosom.'

This time, even Dawson Turner's credulity was stretched
beyond the limit. Was it possible that Manby, without prior
arrangement or invitation, could, in this casual way, have
dropped in on the Duchess of Kent and the heir to the Throne?

Dawson Turner had swallowed a great deal, but he could not swallow this. In his opinion it was all a pack of lies, and he told Manby so in an unusually acid letter. Manby wrote back ,'Your letter gave me no small degree of pain, from your appearing to suspect my account respecting the very flattering interview I received from the Duchess of Kent and Princess Victoria. I trusted that you loved me too much to think I would deceive you in any statement, for anxious as I am to stand fair in history, it shall never be at the expense of truth or by dishonourable fraud.'

It was not quite the end of their long friendship; but it marked the beginning of the end. Was he lying? Was it, perhaps, all an illusion? Or was the grand-daughter of George the Third playing the same cruel sport of Manby-baiting at which her relatives had proved so adept? One thing is certain, if Manby deceived others, he also deceived himself. For him it had all happened, exactly as he described. All the hopes that had perished so miserably under three kings, now underwent a miraculous resurrection.

The violent fluctuations in his fortune, the work, the anxiety of the trials, and the excitement—above all, the excitement—proved too much for Manby's health. He could not sleep; he ran a constant fever; he was virtually blind with a recurrence of the eye inflammation. He drove himself on until he collapsed. Captain Hastings discovered him in his lodgings in a state of delirium, and hastily summoned the *Excellent*'s surgeon.

'He gave me blue pills and a strong aperient,' Manby described the treatment, 'the latter every two hours until it operated. The disease kept rising to the eyes. In three hours the bowels were relieved, and I slept. More blue pills and aperient, and now all danger is past, but I must keep to the house for two or three days.'[8]

The surgeon advised Manby to rest and to leave the experiments to Captain Hastings. But while there was life left in Manby, rest was impossible. Even if his body could be forced to a standstill, nothing could stop the feverish activity of his mind.

Already he was planning another visit across the Solent to his friends on the Isle; he was writing an account of the *Excellent* trials to submit to the Royal Society; he was corresponding with Ross, the Arctic explorer, and the Swedish government, about his scheme for an icy convict colony, and he had sent to Yarmouth for his fire cart and extinguishers in preparation for a demonstration in the dockyard.

During the last week of the trials, the Commander-in-Chief, Sir Thomas Williams, joined the officers on the *Excellent*. 'The 32 pounder,' Manby wrote, 'was discharged by the means brought in by me, without the application of fire, to his great astonishment.' But the Commander was even more impressed by the two-shot device and the oblong shell which carried a warhead. 'Manby,' he said, 'you will reduce naval actions from hours to minutes.'

'That, sir,' Manby replied, 'is my intention, and if I live, three decked ships shall be proved useless, and a great saving to the nation obtained, for if my advice is taken, a two-decker shall make any three-decker strike or be struck in five minutes.'[9]

His success was shadowed by an uneasy conscience. The self-accusation that he was a traitor to his own high principles could not be entirely stilled. A correspondent to the *Portsmouth Herald* had written to ask how Captain Manby, the life preserver, could consistently advocate the adoption of life destroying inventions. The editorial answer was that, however anomalous, all life destroyers used in war turned out to be life preservers. This was what Manby had been telling himself, but there were times, particularly during long, sleepless nights, when he knew that the argument was specious and dishonest. He felt an urgent need to justify his ambiguous position.

'I beg most distinctly to state,' he wrote to Dawson Turner, 'that the experiments are from feelings of Patriotism and Humanity—the former to keep pace with foreign maritime nations, and the latter from a confident persuasion that causing vast devastation and destruction in the onset of an action, will not only bring such action to a speedy termination, but lessen loss of life and diminish the miseries of war.'

This sounded well, but for all his vast capacity for self-deception, he was tortured with doubt and anxiety. The surgeon had no pills, of any colour, to resolve the spiritual conflict within him and bring him peace of mind.

It was a relief to turn briefly from guns and destruction, to the preservation of life and property from fire. His equipment had arrived from Yarmouth, and a demonstration of his portable extinguisher took place in the dockyard, before a large crowd of spectators, including the Commander-in-Chief, and Admiral Maitland, the Dockyard Superintendent. An old sentry box, impregnated with pitch, was set up on trestles and ignited. When the fire was blazing fiercely, a dockyard fireman trundled up with Manby's fire cart, and attempted to quell the flames with the extinguisher. At first he squirted the fluid everywhere, except in the right direction, convincing Manby that he was deliberately sabotaging the experiment because of the prejudice against his invention held by orthodox firemen. However, once the jet was aimed correctly, the fire was put out almost immediately.

'The unprejudiced,' wrote Manby, 'assured me that nothing could have been more *completely successful*, and a statement in the "Portsmouth Herald" confirmed that fact.'

Admiral Maitland's verdict was: 'Your firecart, Manby, might be used with advantage in the Dockyard, as the cylinder it contains can be brought into action for the extinction of fires in the early stages, much sooner than a fire engine, which requires a number of men to move it to the spot required, and some time to arrange it before it can act. But,' he added, 'I do not think it would have much effect in extinguishing a fire that had gained any strength.'[10]

Manby was satisfied, for it was for the very purpose of preventing fires gaining any strength that his extinguisher had been designed. He had for years contended that large fires could only be effectively dealt with by a properly trained, well organised and state supported brigade.

At the end of November he was back in London. Reports on the gunnery experiments had gone to the Admiralty for evaluation.[11] Manby was supremely confident. He had no doubt in his mind that the Navy would immediately be re-equipped with his revolutionary inventions, thus giving England absolute mastery of the seas. Fame and fortune were virtually within his grasp, but, just for the moment, he was a little short of money.

'There has not been the slightest expense relating to the experiments aboard the "Excellent",' he explained to Dawson Turner, 'but those relating to fire have been entirely out of my own pocket, which obliges me to request Ten pounds . . .'

The banker sent the money; but his reluctance was beginning to show. His letters to Manby no longer started 'My dearest Friend'; now they were addressed to 'Dear Captain Manby'. Soon this was to become 'Dear Sir', and finally, before the letters ceased altogether, 'Sir'.

Manby always thought of himself as a young man, full of promise. He could not understand that to other people, promise was not enough in a man of sixty-eight, and that youth had definitely gone.

8

MANBY'S PLAN[1] FOR an efficiently organised, publicly financed fire brigade was so far in advance of his time, that it is only in recent years that it has been fully implemented. The Insurance Offices had clearly failed, and so had the new Water Companies, which had undertaken to provide ready supplies of high pressure water. Something new and revolutionary was clearly required. The need was obvious; the toll taken by fire in lives and property was horrifying, while the existing methods served only to aggravate the problem.

'Confusion upon confusion,' Manby wrote. 'Human efforts expended in spots where they are of no use. The flames consuming everything that is precious or sacred without the possibility of checking them, for want of well-arranged and preconcerted arrangements—for want, in one word, of an organised National Fire Police.'

Manby's plan, carefully thought out down to the last detail, was specifically for London, but it was equally valid for any large city. The first step was to buy the existing engines and equipment from the insurance companies. Manned fire stations were then to be built 'in suitable and perspicacious situations', with engines and horses ready for immediate service. To overcome the shortage of water, and the dependence for supplies on the river, he proposed building eight reservoirs at strategic points. The firemen, instead of being watermen employed on a casual basis, were to be full-time professionals. They were to be called 'The British Firemen', and Manby suggested the most suitable men—cool and daring, able to cope with fire and water—would be ex-sailors.

Each engine was to have a crew appointed to it, responsible for its upkeep and operation, while the firemen were to be given smart uniforms, designed to resist fire and be readily distinguishable at night. There was to be a Director in overall charge, a scientific department to study the causes of fires and methods of prevention and a corps of officers to take command. These 'commanding superintendents' were to appear at the scene of a fire mounted and in uniform. Manby even designed the badges that would be awarded for good conduct and enterprise, one, for those who especially distinguished themselves, resembling the Legion of Honour.

It was an excellent plan; but it was also very expensive. The country was in desperate economic straits, and not only was it a bad moment to ask the Treasury to take on the burden of fire brigades but since no particular government department was responsible, it seemed impossible to arouse official interest.

There seemed to Manby to be one faint gleam of hope. A Parliamentary Committee was about to sit to examine the organisation of the Police, and by the simple semantic device of calling his firemen Fire Police, he might creep within the Committee's terms of reference. He printed an illustrated pamphlet setting out his plans, and sent copies to all the members of the

Portrait in oils of Manby by Sir Thomas Lawrence

Dawson Turner

Volunteers parading at Great Yarmouth

Police Committee, three hundred other M.P.s, and everyone else he could think of who might have the slightest influence. He haunted the Home Office, demanding an interview with Lord Melbourne. Melbourne's secretary palmed him off with an introduction to Colonel Rowan, the Head Commissioner of Police. Rowan asked him to lunch, and was very polite.

'He warmly approved my productions,' Manby wrote,[2] 'and this I shall communicate to Lord M. I have not time to state the flattering opinion he formed of my labours.' But when he managed to see the chairman of the Committee, a man called Carter, his reception was not so encouraging. There was no possibility, Carter said, of his Committee considering Manby's plan. His instructions were to enquire into the state of the Police, and this had nothing whatever to do with fire.

Manby tried desperately to find an M.P. willing to move in the House for an extension of the Committee's powers. He found one at last at a dinner given by the Royal National Institution. This dinner, Sir James Graham,[3] the First Lord, presiding, seemed to Manby yet another of those occasions which were the most important in his life. Apart from finding a sponsor for his Motion, the First Lord proposed his toast 'in strains of eloquence impossible to express, confirming that nothing is so touching to the human heart as that of praise'.

Manby was quite overcome by the First Lord's flattery. He wept openly. Had he known the Judas role Graham was eventually to play in putting paid to his most cherished hopes, he might have wept for a different reason. When he had recovered sufficiently, he rose to reply, comparing the National Society with certain others with which he had been connected—societies 'riddled with the baneful influence of *prejudice*—a word hateful to me, but which I hope from the spirit of the time will be rooted out'. He had written, he told the guests, and intended to publish, an important address to the British Nation on this subject.

Now that he was on his feet in front of so distinguished an

audience, and aware that gentlemen of the press were busily making notes at the remoter tables, the opportunity to further ingratiate himself with the next Monarch was too good to miss. It was the Duke of Kent, he said, who had first encouraged his experiments. He had left behind an illustrious daughter, born to reign over the destinies of the Nation, and who would know how much that nation owed to sailors. He trusted, therefore, that the present occasion was not inappropriate to propose the health of Princess Victoria.[4] Appropriate or not, it was certainly tactless, and must finally have put paid to any chance that was left of finding favour in the eyes of William the Fourth.

After the dinner, he caught a chill, which left him with a cough and a pain in the chest so distressing that he was advised 'to leave Town with precipitation'. He wrote to Dawson Turner that he was coming back to Yarmouth. He had reason to believe that the utmost of his wishes were to be fulfilled, not only regarding the Fire Police, but also in other ways, for Sir James Graham had told him that the Admiralty intended to recommend him to the King for some testimony of Royal bounty. Meanwhile, would his friend tell his wife that he was coming, and to have mutton broth ready for him?

Yarmouth was no longer home for Manby. The local people looked upon him with suspicion and mistrust, and even to his own wife he was now a stranger. In the small, provincial community, everyone knew his business—how much he owed the butcher, how the Barrack Sergeant had assumed the Master's duties, how it was only Dawson Turner who was keeping him out of the debtors' prison, and only his brother-in-law who prevented him from squandering his neglected wife's tiny patrimony. Sir Thomas Gooch lost no chance to add coals to the fire. His malice was tireless and unmerciful, and there was always the fatal, poisonous grain of truth in his calumnies.

Manby rarely went outside the Barracks; even more rarely was he invited to do so. He closeted himself in his room, isolated, lonely, becoming daily more introverted and peculiar. Surrounded by his papers, his models and his medals, he worked ceaselessly on his inventions, projects, plans and pamphlets, creating a world of his own where it was all of vital importance. Much of it *was* important, so obviously important to Manby that there could only be one reason why the outside world refused to recognise his genius. The insidious influence of prejudice could be detected everywhere. Exactly who was prejudiced, or why, he did not know. He was fighting an invisible enemy; a secret society, whose members never showed their faces.

After so many disappointments, most men verging on seventy would have given up the struggle. But to Manby giving up was death. He was now an irredeemable addict, and the drug was a terrible mixture of praise and hope. Praise, no matter where it came from, or how insincere, was as essential to him as air, while before his eyes all the time was a mirage of fame and honour.

It was only in London that he could obtain his peculiar opium in sufficient doses. At all costs, he had to get back to London, to the excitement, the activity that seemed so portentous and the illusion that he was part of the great world of affairs.

The fruits of his solitude in Yarmouth were two new inventions. One was a chemical process for fireproofing women's clothing, a useful exercise, worthy but uninspired. The other was one of those brilliant strokes of genius which redeemed all his faults and foolishness, and alone would have entitled him to everlasting fame. Like all his ideas, it was simple—anyone *could* have thought of it, but no one else had.

The idea concerned lighthouses. At that time, lighthouses were merely beacons set up to warn sailors of the existence of a hazard. There was nothing to distinguish one from the other. Manby's plan was that every lighthouse should send out its own identifying signal, thus enabling ships to obtain an immediate and accurate check on their position. It does not need to be said that this is the system now in use throughout the world. Needless to say, too, Manby has received no credit for it.

In May he returned to London, taking lodgings in Lambeth to be near a model-maker and mechanic with whose assistance, he told Dawson Turner, 'I have produced a most important advance in rendering female dresses incombustible, and whose aid is required in arranging my grand design not only for the improvement of lighthouses, but distinguishing every light by change of mutations.'

This time, he told the banker, he did not intend to leave London until his services had been brought before the public. Life was so hectic, he was too tired to write to his wife, but he trusted his friend to enquire in what manner he could contribute to her comfort and happiness.

On June 13th, Admiral Thomas Manby killed himself by taking an overdose of opium in a bedroom of the George Hotel, Southampton. For many years he had been suffering from the effects of yellow fever contracted in the West Indies; he had also received several serious wounds in action. Opium, taken at first to relieve pain, had become an addiction, and an escape from the disappointments and frustrations of his life. Although the Admiral had done well financially out of his service in the Navy, and had augmented his personal fortune by marrying a rich woman, money could not compensate for the spite and enmity of the Royal Family, which had robbed him of the honours less distinguished officers than himself had been awarded as a matter of course.

His brother's death was a great shock to Manby. He was now the last surviving male member of the family, and the duty of arranging the funeral and looking after the widow and her two daughters fell upon his inadequate shoulders. In the event, Mrs Admiral Manby proved quite capable of looking after herself, but the funeral was a different matter. Manby always loyally main-

tained that his brother's death had been accidental; but few
people shared this kindly view. The rector at Southampton
refused to allow the burial to take place in any hallowed ground
under his jurisdiction, and Manby had the unpleasant task of
touting for a clergyman willing to accept his brother's body.
Eventually the Admiral was buried in the little churchyard at
Itchen, 'a very beautiful and picturesque spot beside the river,'
Manby told Dawson Turner, 'where the parson is free from ridiculous scruples'.

After the funeral, Mrs Manby and her daughters decamped
immediately for the Continent, while Manby, instead of returning
to London, felt compelled to re-visit the scenes of his youth, and
to make a sentimental pilgrimage to his old home at Hilgay. The
expedition was a mistake, and brought only a sharpened sense of
exclusion and loneliness. The people who now owned the house
were total strangers; nevertheless, they treated Manby with great
civility and invited him to stay the night. He was given the room
in which his mother had died—it was as long ago as 1783, but he
remembered it clearly.

Wood Hall was full of ghosts for Manby. Through his bedroom
window he could see across the meadows to the little church with
its avenue of limes. Once he had sat in the squire's pew with his
father, and later, he had sat there as squire in his own right, with
a beautiful young bride beside him. Where he would die, he did
not know, but it would not be in the peace of a country house,
securely enclosed by his own lands. The feeling of dispossession
was unbearable as he sat down to write to Dawson Turner. He
had decided that he would at least be buried at Hilgay. He remembered he had already given away his head, so, he wrote, 'I will
address the Lord of the Manor asking permission to lay my head-
less trunk in the chancel by my father's side.'

That October, while Manby was still living in Lambeth, an
event took place which demonstrated in a most dramatic way the

need for his Fire Police. On the evening of October 17th the Houses of Parliament, both Lords and Commons, were burnt to the grounds.

Manby was eating his dinner when he heard a cry of 'Fire!' This cry, he told Dawson Turner, 'always calls the energies of my mind to action'. From the window of his room he could see down Paris Street across the river to Westminster. He looked out and saw 'the whole space to be decried between the two sides of the street in one awful, raging sheet of fire'. He abandoned his dinner at once, and hurried out to join the fast-increasing procession making its way eagerly towards Westminster Bridge.

Fire watching was a recognised public entertainment, and the fascination of the pastime seemed to thrive on familiarity. Crowds sprang from nowhere to watch quite modest fires, while a really spectacular blaze soon attracted a vast mob. Frequently what had started as passive fire-watching developed into a minor civil war, when troops were called out to force a passage for the fire engines and to repress violence and looting.

Out in the street, Manby could see on the far side of the river a lurid pillar of flame rising from the Palace of Westminster, and an immense cloud of ruddy smoke billowing above it. The brilliance of the flames lit up the river which was jammed with an armada of boats and barges, loaded to the water with sightseers. When Manby reached Westminster Bridge he found it blocked by a solid mass of spectators. The atmosphere was festive; no one seemed perturbed that the seat of the law makers was being destroyed; many seemed happily convinced that the laws would perish with the buildings, and showed every intention of keeping the blaze going as long as possible. Every time a shower of sparks burst from the roof, or flames exploded from a window, cheers of delight and encouragement went up.

Manby fought his way across the bridge, determined, he said, 'to see where I could be most useful'; but when he witnessed the total chaos reigning on the Westminster side of the river, he realised that there was nothing he, or anyone else, could do. The fire, which had started in a lobby of the House of Lords, had spread quickly to the Commons, and was now threatening the Speaker's house and Westminster Hall. Manby arrived on the scene just as the roof of the Commons fell in with a noise like the discharge of heavy guns. Immediately a rumour spread through the crowd that a magazine of gunpowder had been ignited and was about to blow up, and there was panic as those in the forefront tried to escape.

A regiment of Grenadier Guards had been deployed to protect the firemen and to assist in manning the pumps; but as far as Manby could see, only two engines were actually in operation, and these were too far away to have any noticeable effect on the inferno. It was impossible to bring the engine any closer because it was low tide, and the intake hoses were too short to reach the river.

There appeared to be no one in command to direct operations, and the unco-ordinated efforts of firemen and soldiers merely added to the confusion and the dangers. The situation was scarcely improved by the arrival of three regiments of Horse Guards and a miscellaneous fleet of carts, coaches and hackney cabs, hired, it was said, by Lord Melbourne to remove documents and books to a place of safety. The Horse Guards were put to work clearing furniture out of the Law Courts and the Speaker's house. Their efforts tended to become erratic, if not hilarious, when they discovered the Speaker possessed a well-stocked cellar.

It was a night of many casualties. Several firemen were buried in the rubble of collapsing walls, and numerous spectators were burnt or trampled on. Manby himself narrowly escaped being run over by a fire engine. He jumped out of the way, and in doing so, put his knee out of joint. 'I had just power,' he told Dawson Turner, 'to reach some iron railings, to which I clung until a Good Samaritan came to my aid. He helped me to Old Palace Yard, put me in a cab and left before I could get his name.

As the cab drove off I caught a glimpse through the great doors of Westminster Hall. The fierce light of the fire reflected through the great windows at the end, exhibited a splendour awfully grand.'

It seemed to Manby impossible that Parliament, when it found somewhere unburnt to sit, would not now give whole-hearted support for his Fire Police. His hopes were supported by the outcry in the newspapers, roundly condemning the inefficiency of the existing system. 'There is a total lack of direction,' wrote *The Times*. 'Each fire office acts according to its own view. There is no obedience to one chief, and consequently where the completest co-operation is needed, all is confusion and contradiction.'

Manby's knee kept him indoors for several days, but as soon as he was able he limped to see Colonel Rowan. The Colonel admitted that there 'was a want of union among persons in the direction of Fire Engines,' and provided Manby with a police escort to view the ruins of the Palace of Westminster. From among the ashes, Manby retrieved the charred fragment of an order paper, which he sent to Dawson Turner as a souvenir. Dawson Turner filed the scrap of paper meticulously, and it still survives in the Wren Library at Cambridge.

Since his brother's death, Manby had had little contact with his sister-in-law or his two nieces. They belonged to a world as remote from his own as the moon. They were smart, sophisticated, cosmopolitan; perhaps the only thing they had in common with Manby was the disfavour of the Royal Family.

The elder girl, who had married the Barronne de Feuchères's nephew, and had become the Countess de Flassons, was now a widow. The Count had died in mysterious circumstances; it was rumoured he had been poisoned, and at a later stage the Barronne was to be accused of his murder. The Countess had inherited the fortune and estates which had been lavished upon her husband by the Prince. She had also acquired the arrogance of wealth, and all the airs and graces of an aristocrat in a country that was still basically feudal. The younger niece, Georgina, was beautiful, headstrong and spoiled. Manby was proud of his baroque relations; he liked to boast about them, and to read about them in the gossip columns; but they remained as distant and unreal as the characters of a romantic novel.

In the spring of 1835, Mrs Admiral Manby, in Rome with Georgina, was taken seriously ill. Convinced she was about to die, she came home to London. The elegant town house in Montague Street was opened to receive her. The Countess was summoned from France, and Manby from his humble lodgings in Lambeth. On her deathbed, Manby's sister-in-law entrusted him, as her husband's nearest surviving relative, with the care of her daughters, and made him an executor of her estate. For weeks she hovered between life and death. Manby sent regular bulletins to Dawson Turner, writing them, with macabre economy, on the black-margined paper of which he had prudently laid in a large supply.

'Although my paper would denote the awful crisis had taken place,' he wrote, 'yet it is not so, for she still breathes. Her life is suspended by a thread. I have seen her; but she is totally insensible.'

His elder niece, he said, impressed him greatly with her character and power of mind. She had begged him to be her adviser. As for Georgina, it was clear she would need affectionate firmness in handling. Already he was feeling the weight of his unaccustomed responsibilities.

Mrs Manby died, and the funeral paper could be put to its proper use. Mrs Manby had wished to be buried with her husband in the village churchyard beside the River Itchen. This entailed a long and complicated journey, with hearse, coffin and mourners which started from Montague Street in torrential rain. The rain continued for two days, soaking to the skin the strangely assorted party at the graveside.

The funeral over, Manby was faced with problems for which he was wholly unfitted and unprepared. It was a daunting situation to find himself *in loco parentis* to two young women. He was seventy; he had never been a father, and, despite two marriages, he had lived a solitary life concerned exclusively with his own affairs. It would have been difficult enough if they had been ordinary young women, not a French countess and a wilful, strong-willed beauty of eighteen, who had been accustomed to having her own way in every detail. They were both used to life in the grand manner, on a scale inconceivable to their uncle; equally inconceivable to them was Manby's hand to mouth existence. Just how remote they were from the reality of Yarmouth, was clearly shown when they casually told Manby they had decided to reside with him for a time. They would bring their own servants, and an elderly couple who had been faithful retainers of their parents. 'This will need some alterations to my personal establishment,' Manby wrote to Dawson Turner. The understatement masked a note of panic.

Sophia was even more inadequate than Manby. She had lived too long a virtual recluse, with the aged and eccentric Frost as her only companion. Retirement had been forced upon her almost from the first day of her marriage, and it was too late now for her to emerge as manager and hostess. She remained in the background, uncomplaining and uncomprehending, while Manby turned everything upside down in a frantic effort to transform the gloomy barrack house into a fitting residence for two fashionable young women and their retinue. There was an empty house next door, and Manby persuaded the Barrack Board to grant him the lease. Local tradesmen, suddenly accommodating, provided furniture on credit; the Countess and her sister, their servants and their mountains of luggage moved in.

It was an arrangement that could not last. The daughters of Admiral Manby were as out of their element on the bleak east coast as tropical birds. It was all so cold; all so dull and provincial. Manby did his best, and so too, in her feeble way, did Sophia; but as soon as the first shock of grief at their mother's death had worn off, the girls became restless and bored. The Countess found that urgent business recalled her to France, while Georgina, who had only come to life when dashing young officers had been present, accepted with alacrity an invitation to stay with the Barronne de Feuchères.

The Barracks returned to gloom, solitude and poverty. The tradesmen who had been so delighted to serve the Countess and her sister, ceased to be obliging. And now, to add to his financial burdens, Manby had an unoccupied house, full of expensive furniture, to pay for.

9

THE MODERN VERSION of Manby's line-throwing apparatus is nowadays operated by the Coastguard Service.[1] Although the principle remains unchanged, many improvements have been made over the years, and a greatly increased range and accuracy has been achieved by replacing the mortar with cordite rockets.

The use of rockets had been suggested from the earliest days of the invention. Manby, who resented the rocket-makers trespassing on what he considered his private territory, always opposed the idea, and treated with scorn all attempts to develop this method of projecting the line.

Manby's most formidable rival was a man called John Dennett. Working on the Isle of Wight, Dennett had already saved several lives with a form of Manby's apparatus powered with a rocket. He was sponsored by Captain Harris, a retired naval officer who owned one of the principal rope making factories in the world— the Colonial Ropery at Grimsby. In the autumn of 1835, Captain

Harris invited Manby and Dennett to take part in a public trial, Manby pitting his mortar against Dennett's rocket. Captain Harris suggested that the beach at Skegness would be a suitable place for the contest; he would provide the ropes and defray all expenses.

Manby viewed the challenge with mixed feelings. On one hand, his sporting instincts were aroused, and how wonderful it would be if his mortar thoroughly punished the upstart rocket; on the other, suppose the inconceivable happened, and he were to lose? The prospect was really too dreadful to contemplate. Dawson Turner told him it would be undignified to take part, but Manby, who could not bear anyone to think he was afraid of the outcome, picked up the gauntlet.

The first week in September he travelled to Grimsby across the great embankment which had just been completed, connecting Norfolk with Lincoln. He stayed with Captain Harris, the promoter, who seemed determined to treat the whole affair as though it were a prize fight. It pleased Manby to find himself regarded as the reigning champion, and Dennett as the contender. A committee of local sportsmen were in charge of the arrangements, and there was a panel of referees.

The organisation and the advance publicity were both thoroughly professional, and on the day of the event it appeared to Manby that all the County of Lincolnshire had congregated on the seafront at Skegness. Several marquees had been set up, in one of which an elegant lunch was served. To his delight, Manby found himself surrounded by a bevy of elegantly dressed and admiring ladies. There were speeches and toasts, while outside on the beach an excited crowd gathered expectantly round the roped enclosure where the rival machines had been installed ready for the first round.

After lunch, the committee and the contestants retired to the judges' tent to arrange the order of firing and other details. Manby, as champion, was given the choice whether or not he would go first; but he had already decided on an attitude of *noblesse oblige*, and said he would allow Mr Dennett to make any arrangements he might think proper.

'This obtained for me the highest praise from all present,' he told Dawson Turner, 'and especially from Mr Dennett, who expressed it as most liberal.'

Dennett decided to fire first, and the contestants, accompanied by the committee, the judges and a party of workmen equipped with measuring chains, made their way down to the beach where they were greeted with loud cheers.

The conditions were perfect; a bright, autumn afternoon with very little wind. If anything, the weather favoured the rocket, for the heavier mortar shot would have had an undoubted advantage had it been gusty or raining; but it was not Dennett's lucky day. His first rocket merely fizzed, and refused to leave the ground; his second took off splendidly, but suddenly changed its course in mid-flight and plummetted straight into the beach. His best attempt only carried the rope a distance of two hundred yards. For Manby everything went without a hitch. His mortar did not fail once, and one shot went over a quarter of a mile, more than twice his rival's best.

It was a triumphant victory, and Manby's joy was childish and extreme. Tears streamed down his face as he acknowledged the applause of the crowd. His feelings, he wrote to Dawson Turner that night, were impossible to be explained. His heart was bursting with joy, and he regarded this as the proudest day of his life.

Mr Dennett had been a most gentlemanly opponent, and Manby could not help feeling sorry for him. 'I assure you,' he wrote, 'the ill-success that attended the rocket generally, gave me ideas of the feelings of Mr Dennett.'

Now that the challenger had been counted out, Manby could afford to be magnanimous. In the presence of the judges, he complimented Dennett on his efforts, and even went so far as to admit that there might be occasions when a rocket could be more advantageously applied than a mortar. Although, for the moment, the mortar had been vindicated, Manby had seen enough to know in his heart that the future lay with the rocket. On the principle that if he could not beat them, he had better join them, he invited his rival to Yarmouth 'to assist', he said, 'in discovering the cause of the failure of the rocket, so truly unfortunate to-day'.[2]

Early in 1836, both Manby's wife and the Barronne de Feuchères fell ill. Manby, like many people who themselves have suffered a great deal, was inclined to regard other people's complaints as affectation. Involved as he was in a daily struggle against blinding headaches, rheumatism, failing eyesight and insomnia, he had no patience with sick people. His wife had ceased to expect sympathy or comfort from her husband. She suffered in silence. 'Mrs Manby is ill,' he wrote to Dawson Turner, 'but she is quiet, and gives neither me nor her attendant Frost the least trouble.'

The Barronne, on the other hand, was far from quiet, and gave everyone the maximum trouble. Since her lover, the Prince de Condé, had hanged himself with a cravat from the handle of a window at the Château St Leu, the Barronne had been the centre of one of the longest and most complicated lawsuits in the history of French jurisprudence. The point at issue was whether the Prince's will, leaving his fortune to the Barronne, was legal. In the course of the proceedings, the Barronne's past had been revealed in all its scandalous details; she had been accused of every kind of vice and crime, including the murder of the Prince and of her nephew, the Count de Flassons. Although nothing was ever proved against her, and in the end she succeeded in establishing her right to the bulk of the Bourbon wealth, feeling against her for a time ran so high in France that she was obliged to seek sanctuary in her native country. Here, at least, she had one friend whose loyalty was unassailable.

Manby invited the Barronne to Yarmouth, but like previous

visitors, she soon tired of the dull and narrow life at the Barracks. She preferred to stay in London, occupying a suite at the Bath Hotel. Manby called on her frequently, and when she was ill, he was the first person she summoned to her bedside. Manby did not think it despicable, or even peculiar, that he should eagerly attend the Barronne in a London hotel, while his own wife lay lonely and neglected at Yarmouth. Sophia was merely indisposed; the Barronne was acting out a great drama. Manby loved drama as much as he detested sickness. The Barronne's illness was important; millions of francs hung in the balance; half the crowned heads of Europe watched her progress with bated breath. Yarmouth seemed a long way away when he held the fabulous courtesan's fevered hand, and felt the fat Bourbon diamonds cutting into his palm.

As rumours of the Barronne's putative crimes circulated, Manby defended her valiantly in numerous letters to the newspapers. His loyalty paid handsome dividends in the form of publicity. At the time of the Barronne's illness, he was delivering a series of lectures, combined with an exhibition of his models, at the Adelaide Gallery. No previous lectures had been so well attended, or aroused so much interest from the press. The editors of the *Morning Post*, the *Morning Herald* and *The Age*, all sought him out for an interview. Mr Westamacott of *The Age*, in the omniscient manner of editors, promised he would personally bring Manby's services before the King, while the *Morning Post* gave him a most flattering notice, rebuking the government for their neglect, while honouring inferior persons.

But newspaper editors, for all their fine words and grand promises, did not make out the Honours List, and Manby's association with the notorious Barronne was looked upon by those who did with disapproval. Lord John Russell, the current Home Secretary, to whom Manby wrote claiming some mark of Royal recognition, did not reply. Manby asked Dawson Turner to draft for him 'a firm, dignified and manly request to be informed

Two of the prints presented by Manby to Queen Victoria on her coronation

Manby in 1832

what part of my conduct caused the refusal to place my services before the King, in view of the elevated opinion in which I am held in every nation except my own'.

That year a Committee of the House of Commons sat to consider the building of an Eastern Railway. The exact route this railway was to take and, even more important, the place where it was to terminate, aroused fierce local rivalries, for railways brought with them trade, industry and prosperity. Manby appointed himself as champion of Yarmouth as Terminus and Packet Station, and gave evidence which, he wrote, greatly impressed the Committee. The Chairman paid him particular attention, and assured him his opinions carried considerable weight.[3]

It hurt Manby that his efforts were not so well received in Yarmouth itself. The Mayor, in particular, resented his interference, and publicly repudiated him as the town's spokesman. But he had become accustomed to the mean, grovelling minds of local dignitaries, and he could take a haughty view of their envious spite now that the Lord Mayor of London had invited him to the Mansion House. It was highly gratifying, Manby wrote,[4] to receive the compliments of the Chief Magistrate of the Metropolis, and to be asked by him to be the founder of a Society for the Prevention of Fire. The Lord Mayor, in reality, merely asked Manby if he would give a lecture at a meeting that was being arranged to consider the possibility of forming such a Society; but, in Manby's mind, it was an insignificant step from this to the conviction that he had been entrusted with its entire organisation. The Society, he told Dawson Turner, would be an imperishable monument to his name, and this being the case, he decided, quite independently, that it should be a Royal one. He drew up a petition which he took with him to Buckingham Palace. He sent in his card, endorsed 'Captain Geo. W. Manby, to present a Petition praying His Majesty to become the patron of a Society formed for the rescue of life from houses in flames, and conferring on it the title "Royal" '. After a long wait in an anteroom, he was seen by a secretary, who 'intimated the matter should have attention'. Manby seemed to have imagined that he might be summoned there and then for an interview with the King, in the manner of his encounter with the Duchess of Kent. 'I passed on as fast as I could,' he wrote, 'with a thankful feeling I was not desired to kneel down.'[5]

Having delivered this petition, Manby behaved as though the request had been granted. Palace officials were justifiably annoyed, and Manby received a sharp letter of rebuke, pointing out that his petition was still under consideration by the Home Office, and expressing surprise at the way he had jumped the gun. Undeterred, Manby used the prefix 'Royal' when he wrote to Russell and Peel, setting forth the services he had rendered the State, and asking their support for the new Society, and did nothing to discourage his editor friends from referring to the latest Royal Society.

Manby's hopes were in the ascendant. 'I have strong reason to think,' he wrote, 'that the day is very near when my services are no longer overlooked, not only in a pecuniary way, but in elevation of rank.'[6] It was unfortunate that Dawson Turner should have chosen this crucial moment to place an embargo on further borrowing. In future, he told Manby, the bank would be unable to accommodate him beyond twenty pounds. 'This obliges me to avoid rank, if possible,' Manby replied, 'on the honourable grounds that I cannot afford the fees. I must be given credit for integrity, and I have the feeling that the name of Captain Manby will be better known and more highly appreciated than that of Sir George Manby.' The tone of his letter was reproachful. 'I am ashamed,' he wrote, 'to contemplate self-destitution, and the feeling that I have no friend to relieve my present want.'

He was surrounded by creditors; he owed so much to so many people, he had lost track of the details. Although he was convinced he would soon be in greater opulence than ever before, the spectre of the debtors' prison grew daily more menacing.

Although Manby was too self-centred to realise it, Sophia suffered more than he did from the miseries of poverty. It was she who endured a state of siege at Yarmouth, who suffered the insults and threats of unpaid tradesmen; who dared not show her face outside the Barracks because of the whispers and the gossip. In desperation, she swallowed her pride, overcame her timidity and appealed for help to an old friend of the Gooch family. He replied: 'any cheque you draw will be honoured'. Manby immediately took advantage of this ill-advised generosity, by drawing one for fifty pounds.

The ceaseless activity of chasing shadows in so many directions generated the illusion that at any moment something tangible would materialise in his grasp. He was no longer sure what that something would be, for his purpose had become diffused and uncertain. In June, however, a Motion came before the House of Commons, which brought his aims sharply into focus. James Silk Buckingham,[7] a member whose advanced views and zeal for radical reform were a constant irritant to the government, moved successfully for a committee to enquire whether the loss of life and property from shipwreck could not be greatly reduced. At last, it seemed to Manby, his great opportunity had arrived. His services must now inevitably be brought into prominence and properly evaluated, for how could such an enquiry ignore his achievements, or even function at all without his expert evidence and advice? It was another shadow; but a shadow that seemed deceptively substantial. Buckingham, he told Dawson Turner, had received his offer of assistance with great eagerness. 'I tell you in confidence, and without vanity, that *I will shine*. I am to have a regular summons to attend the first meeting of the Committee, which takes place in July.'

Apart from anything else, the Committee would give him an excellent excuse for staying in London. Neither Dawson Turner nor the Barrack Board could oppose a summons from the House of Commons; but, for the time being, he was obliged to return to Yarmouth. Before he left, he looked in at the Adelaide Gallery to see how his exhibition was going. He was gratified at the number of visitors, among whom were two Persian princes and their suite. At least, to Manby they were Persian princes. They were handsome men, he told Dawson Turner, who seemed, for some reason, to be much amused.

10

THE GLOOM OF the Barracks was in some measure relieved that summer by a small legacy which came to Manby's wife. The vigilant Gooches saw to it that Manby could not touch the principal, which, apart from repaying the fifty pounds borrowed in Sophia's name, was sunk in an annuity. The income—£120 a year—was insignificant compared with Manby's debts; but it exerted a powerful effect on his behaviour. The money gave him an euphoric illusion of affluence, which led him to act as though large sums were at his disposal. Instead of paying off his debts, he increased them recklessly.

When he returned to London, convinced that he could now afford to live in a more fitting style, he took a suite of rooms in the Adelphi. Three delightful rooms, he told Dawson Turner, overlooking the Thames, at a very reasonable rent which included attendance. He signed the lease for a year. The landlord, Mr Allenby, seemed at the time to be a most charming person, quite overcome at the honour of having so distinguished a tenant.

Buckingham's Committee heard Manby's evidence at the end of July. 'I rejoice to tell you it was most satisfactory,' Manby wrote to his friend, 'and has great importance to self, as I made it the vehicle to lay before the public my past services, to produce for me that which a prejudiced set of persons have withheld for services rendered to the State.'

He confined his evidence to the saving of life, and to the provision of lighthouses; he had been dissuaded from his original intention, which was to reveal to the Committee his ideas on salvaging sunken vessels. For some years, Manby had been studying the technical problems of salvage, and had made calculations which convinced him that the value of sunken property which could be recovered was enormous. He had divulged his findings confidentially to a member of the Committee, who was also a wealthy shipowner, Mr G. F. Young. Young was impressed; his shrewd business instincts told him there might be money to be made from exploiting Manby's ideas commercially.

'I gave my opinion to Mr Young that the matter should be left to the Government,' Manby told Dawson Turner, 'but Mr Young said "decidedly not", as they would consult their own patronage rather than the object contemplated.'

Manby was doubtful. Young, besides being a shipowner, also had substantial interests in insurance. It was impossible not to suspect his motives; on the other hand, it was very flattering to have so rich and important a man pay him so much attention. In the end, Manby compromised; he would keep the salvage scheme secret for the time being while Young and his associates explored the best means of putting it into effect.

While the Committee was sitting, Manby heard from his niece Georgina, still in France with the Barronne, that she had fallen in love and wished to marry. Since she was a minor, Manby's permission as her guardian was required. On the face of things, it seemed an admirable match. The man with whom Georgina appeared completely infatuated was Sir Cavendish Rumbold; he belonged to an aristocratic expatriate family, and his grandfather was Sir William Sidney Smith.[1] Unfortunately, the young man's reputation was unsavoury in the extreme. From all Manby had heard, he was not only dissolute and ·dishonest, but was also involved in dangerous political intrigue. Manby was worried and confused. The responsibility for his young niece's future was one he was too selfish, too innocent and too ignorant to bear alone. He sought advice from those he imagined to have worldly knowledge and sound judgment, with the result that he became more worried and confused than before. Dawson Turner had no doubt that the man was a scoundrel, and the marriage could only end in disaster. The Barronne not only approved the match—she had, after all, probably engineered it—but sent a glowing testimonial to Sir Cavendish's excellence—his charm, wealth and sincere love for Georgina.

The problem of Georgina had its brighter side; it gave him an excuse for another visit to France. Under the circumstances, even Dawson Turner could hardly fail to agree that it was imperative to be on the spot, and, incidentally, give him a substantial advance. It was an opportunity Manby had been longing for. He was convinced that he had only to set foot on French soil for the French government to award him the Legion of Honour. Since his presentation to King Charles the Tenth several more of his essays had been published in translation, he had been elected a member of the Society of Physicals and Chemicals, and had also been invested with the rather spurious title, of which he was immensely proud, of Professor of the Society of the Union of Nations (British Section). This Society, of shaky French origin and mysterious finances, had as its declared purpose the fostering of universal friendship and co-operation in art and science. Manby innocently accepted it at its face value, and was completely taken in by its pretensions. He hoped to use the Society as a medium for the international adoption of his shore-to-ship apparatus, and when he went to France to settle Georgina's problems, he decided to take the line and mortar with him. He hoped to give a series of demonstrations, including throwing a line across the Seine.

This plan, and indeed every other plan, very nearly came to an abrupt end when he was knocked down by a cart while crossing the Strand. The King of the Netherlands was in London on a State visit, and Manby was on his way to thank him personally for the medal the Dutch had given him. Manby was carried unconscious into the house of a nearby doctor, but he came to in time to hear the medical man exclaim: 'Good God, Sir! How extraordinarily prominent is the bump of benevolence on your head!' There was an account of the accident, Manby proudly informed Dawson Turner, in the *Morning Chronicle*. 'Oblige me,' he added, 'by telling Mrs Manby this.'[2]

That August, Manby was busy making preparations for his journey to France. He went to Woolwich 'to give directions for a set of apparatus to be taken with me to Paris, where it is my intention to make a public exhibition across the Seine'. He had a most delightful time at Woolwich. 'I met the pensioners—nothing could be better—and visited each hall where the gallant veterans live. It does highest honour to the Nation. The delight I experienced made tears come into my eyes; but to me, Joy always has that effect.'[3]

He returned to Greenwich by steamer. On the deck he had a rather curious encounter with a fellow traveller who claimed to be French, and further, proved it by handing Manby a bilingual card: 'Mr Louis Fauver, Captain de Guerre, Nobleman.' 'Mr Fauver's delight,' Manby wrote, 'at being acquainted with a man whose name is so much praised, he expressed in the warmest terms. I promised to call upon him and present him with the translated copies of my essay.'

There was another topic, not quite so delightful, which he was obliged to mention to Dawson Turner. 'I look with anxious hope to confer with you on a particular subject,' he wrote, 'that is, hoping you will induce your House to give me some assistance. I feel confident that such a favour cannot long be required. Things are going as prosperously as you could wish.'

Dawson Turner relented to the extent of advancing a quarter's salary, on the condition that Manby returned to England immediately the family business was settled, and at the beginning of September, Manby travelled to France. At Dieppe, the Customs seized and impounded his life-saving apparatus. The import of armaments was forbidden, and as far as the Customs were concerned, this included a mortar with shot and supplies of powder. Manby, hampered by his inability to speak the language, argued in vain. A gun was a gun. *Voilà tout!* If monsieur so desired, he could keep the rope.

It was a bad omen, and set the pattern for a visit during which everything possible seemed to go wrong. Immediately he reached Paris, he found himself the centre of a raging family melodrama which made his brush with Customs seem a minor difference of opinion. Sir Sidney Smith had decided the marriage should not take place. Although Sir Cavendish was his grandson, he was honest enough to admit that he was quite unfit to be a husband. Georgina wept and screamed and threatened to kill herself. It was a situation with which Manby was quite unable to deal. 'I gave the best advice in my power,' he told Dawson Turner.

Georgina, backed by the Barronne de Feuchères, had her way. 'The wedding is to take place on September 15th,' Manby's next letter informed Dawson Turner. 'Afterwards I shall instantly return. It is Sir Cavendish's intention to settle all property he has on my niece. What that property is, God only knows, but on Tuesday next we are to meet his man of law. I cannot but have the strongest apprehension for her future—but she is devoted to him, and he appears to be to her. The wedding is to be on an extensive scale, and after the marriage, she is to take up residence with the Barronne de Feuchères, who is much pleased with Sir Cavendish Rumbold.'

The marriage took place in the State Room of the British Embassy. Georgina was radiant, and Sir Cavendish, on his best behaviour, so elegant and charming that Manby was disarmed. Perhaps, after all, love would triumph, and everything turn out for the best. It was a pious hope, but amid the euphoria of the wedding festivities, seemed to be valid. Manby wore his medals and gave the bride away. The Barronne stage-managed the whole affair most expertly, and after the ceremony, the whole party went to Versailles to speed the couple on their honeymoon.

'Sir Sidney took me there for an excellent meal,' Manby wrote. 'He drank my health in a very flattering way, and said that, despite everything, he was now pleased to be united in relationship to a man whose name stood foremost in the cause of humanity.'

Manby did not keep his promise to return to England immediately after the wedding. Not only was he hoping for an audience with Louis Philippe, the King who had ousted Charles the Tenth in the 1830 revolution,[4] but his presence was also vital to 'rescue the character of the Society for the Union of Nations, and to preserve its original design'. In his absence, the Society had awarded its British Professor a prize of 800 francs for his life-saving efforts, but when he tried to collect the money he was told there were insufficient funds. The finances of the Society were in a most unsatisfactory state, he told Dawson Turner. 'No proper accounts have been kept, and there is a deficiency of 15,000 francs totally unaccounted for. Great credit is due to me for opening the eyes of the Society, and I shall not leave this place until all objectionable parts are removed.'

Dawson Turner sent a scathing reply. He reminded Manby of his undertaking to return to England, and warned him that he was allowing himself to be made the tool of a pack of swindlers.

Manby was 'pained that you attach so little good to the objects of my stay'; but otherwise he ignored both the strictures and the advice. At the same time as Dawson Turner's letter, he received one from the Barrack Sergeant, imploring him to pay immediately tradesmens' bills totalling £19. 13. 9. Proceedings were being threatened, and Mrs Manby was at her wits' end. It seemed to Manby in Paris a trifling sum to make so much fuss about. He was confident his friend would look after everything. 'Have the goodness,' he wrote, 'to advance the Barrack Sergeant the sum he requires. I give you my honour it will be repaid to you.' As an afterthought, he added: 'See my wife, and tell her I am well.'

The leaves fell from the Parisian trees as winter succeeded autumn. Still Manby stayed on in Paris, waiting for a summons from the King; waiting for the Customs to release his apparatus; waiting for the Society to give him his prize; waiting for the Legion of Honour; waiting for a miracle that every day became more improbable. The political situation was confused and tense. At any moment, yet another revolution was expected to depose the Citizen King. The Barronne had transferred a million francs into London banks and had her bags packed ready for instant flight. Under these conditions, to expect anyone to concern themselves with shipwrecked sailors, least of all the King, seemed to be carrying optimism to the point of absurdity.

And then, early in November, it seemed the miracle was about to take place. A letter arrived saying the King would be returning shortly to Paris and would grant Manby an interview. But there was another letter from England, in an uncertain handwriting he hardly recognised. It was from Sophia. She was desperate; for two weeks she had been without a farthing. She had not been able to buy bare necessities, and if it had not been for Frost's tiny savings, which were now nearly exhausted, she would have starved. She begged Manby to come home and relieve her misery.

The letter brought him back to reality with a painful jolt; but what hurt and upset him more than anything was the fact that Dawson Turner had let him down. He contrived to distort the whole affair in his mind, so that Dawson Turner was to blame, not only for Sophia's penury, but also for his extended stay in Paris. He convinced himself that the sole reason for his stay had been to please Dawson Turner by obtaining the Legion of Honour. He did not reply directly to his wife; but he wrote immediately to the banker.

'Proposing my return places me in a difficult position,' he said, 'in my efforts to obtain your wishes. My regret is that my wife did not communicate her wants to you—you would have supplied her, having pledged my honour that it would be returned. My wife's painful situation has defeated the object you were so anxious I should obtain. I shall therefore, with no honour conferred on me, return and appease my wife's feelings. Should you see her, tell her I shall be home on Monday.'

He fully intended at the time to keep his word, but at the last moment he heard a rumour that the King would be in Paris the following day. He unpacked his bags; a day, more or less, after all, could make little difference. He quietened his conscience by sending off to the Barrack Sergeant a draft on Turner's bank for fifty pounds. He could not believe his friend would refuse to honour it.

The King did not return to Paris, nor did Dawson Turner honour the draft. He wrote a severe letter telling Manby that the time had come for plain speaking. Out of compassion for Sophia, he would advance her enough to ensure that she did not starve; but Manby himself must return instantly and concentrate on putting his affairs in order; otherwise he could expect no more help. This time, the limit had definitely been reached.

'There were passages in your last letter,' Manby wrote back, 'that gave me pain. To think that I had not a friend in Yarmouth that would spare the feelings that a few pounds could not be advanced to save my reputation and comfort my wife. As soon as I have seen the King, I shall return, dispose of my property, pay every farthing I owe and myself and my wife will retire to where our names will be honoured.'

Manby himself by this time was practically destitute. The prize of 800 francs from the Society was still unpaid, and likely to remain so. He hung on in Paris for nearly another month; but when in the middle of November the King at last returned and Manby was told to stand by, he was penniless.

'A letter came to say the King will grant me an audience,' he wrote, 'but my finances are getting too low, and I cannot afford the essential costume. I dread travelling, but I must travel without stopping to avoid expense—very hazardous to a man who will be 72 this month. Tell my wife, and inform her of my return.'

At the last minute he changed his plans. Dawson Turner had hardly time to tell Sophia of her husband's homecoming, when another letter arrived from Paris.

'I was too unwell to start Monday,' Manby wrote. 'Severe cold. I will now stay until the summons arrives from the Tuileries, which I hope will not be long. I must put myself under privation to effect an audience—my sole object. I have not been extravagant, but only desire to do good, and leave behind an imperishable name, to be honoured in every civilised part of the globe. I feel that by staying in this country I have effected what no other means could have done. You shall hear from me as soon as I have seen the King. I dread the journey, but hope to eat plum pudding at home on the 25th.'

For another week he waited for the summons from the Tuileries. It did not come. The agitation to depose the King was growing in momentum. Louis Philippe was a virtual prisoner of his own guards, and only those with essential State business were allowed into his presence. Reluctantly, Manby surrendered to the inevitable. There would be no audience. But still he could not entirely give up hope of the decoration he desired so desperately.

'It has been suggested to me that the most effective means of obtaining my great object, and most certain mode of having the Legion of Honour,' he wrote, 'is by Memorial to the King. Perhaps this is wiser than an audience.'

His tiny supply of francs was nearly exhausted. There was now no alternative but to go home. Once in London, he could perhaps raise some money on his medals. He had nothing else.

It was difficult, even for Manby, to delude himself that the French expedition had been anything but a miserable fiasco. But he did his best. His trip, he wrote, had been worth while if only for the great service he had rendered in exposing the malpractices in the Society for the Union of Nations.

'The Society is now in a healthy picture,' he told Dawson Turner, in his final letter from France. 'I have done vast service to subordinates who gave money to support the object of shipwreck, and were duped by artful men. I touched on this in my Memorial to the King.'

11

IN MANBY'S ABSENCE, Sir Thomas Gooch had taken the opportunity to intensify his campaign of vilification. He spread scandalous rumours, which fell on willing ears, and were lent substance and colour by the observable facts that Mrs Manby was destitute, debts were unpaid and Manby had disappeared. Manby, it was said, had shamefully abandoned his wife; he had absconded with the object of cheating his creditors; he was living a life of luxurious immorality with the Barronne de Feuchères; he was a traitor in the pay of the French. The rumours were distorted, enlarged and elaborated as they circulated, so that when Manby did return he found himself notorious. Dawson Turner, although he was now cold and aloof, remained loyal; but his partner behaved in a monstrous manner when Manby called at the bank.

For a time, Manby was obliged to stay at home and practice rigid economy. 'I am struggling to get out of debt,' he wrote. 'I visit no one, I pay for all I have and am devoting myself to prove that I am an honest and honourable man, although unfortunate. Thank God, I have not yet been obliged to raise money on my medals, and I hope there will now be no necessity to.'[1]

Exemplary behaviour such as this could not, and did not last. In March, a quarter's instalment on the annuity fell due. It was not much, but Manby calculated it would support him in London for a month, with enough left over to provide for Sophia's modest needs in Yarmouth. If only he could get to London, he was convinced his fortune would be made. There were so many bright prospects coming into view.

'I left Yarmouth without hope of assistance if destitute,' he wrote, 'but I hope the perseverance which has made me surmount the difficulties of many years will support me. I have endured great sorrows at Yarmouth, the place of all others where I wished to have closed my life. Now I want employment to take me away from the place where I have received so much envy, hatred, malice and all uncharitableness.'[2]

In London, all the shadows he had chased so assiduously before he left for France were waiting to resume the game; and there were new, vigorous illusions eager to join in the fun. First and foremost, there was Buckingham's Bill, awaiting the moment of unveiling. Exactly what the provisions of this Bill would be, Manby did not know—Buckingham had become strangely secretive and elusive—but Manby gathered it was intended to form a Marine Board for the examination of Masters' certificates, the study of ship construction and the improvement of charts and navigation. There was also, he understood, to be a department for the preservation of life from shipwreck, and it was upon this that he pinned his greatest hopes. Clearly, someone would have to be appointed to take charge of the new establishment, and who in the country was better qualified than himself? He decided he must stake his claim at once, and with the maximum publicity.

He ordered a large reprint of his pamphlet *Reflections on Shipwreck*, and he commissioned a series of four engravings illustrating

Lithographs of the wreck of the Killarney Steamer, 1838,
from drawings by William Joy

THE DESTRUCTION by FIRE of the HOUSES of PARLIAMENT

ON THURSDAY NIGHT OCTᴿ 16ᵀᴴ 1834.

his more spectacular rescues. These cost over fifty pounds to produce, but he was certain they would sell splendidly and show a handsome profit. He sent the pamphlet and a set of the engravings to the Duchess of Kent, asking permission to dedicate them to Princess Victoria. He wrote to Lord Palmerston suggesting that his apparatus should be installed in every part of the globe where there was a British Consulate, and he also sent to the Admiralty and to Lloyds a new signal code he had devised to be used with his apparatus. The latest coastguard return had shown that, although seven crews had been saved the previous winter, two had perished because they did not know what to do when the line reached them.

The shipping and insurance interests, led by Mr Young, were strongly opposed to Buckingham's Bill. They dreaded the prospect of a horde of civil servants telling them how to run their business. Manby's plan for raising sunken vessels, however, was a different matter. If a joint stock company were formed for the purpose of saving both property and life at sea, the government would be relieved of expense, the businessmen would be free from interference and there could very well be substantial profits. The idea was undeniably attractive; but was it possible, Manby asked Dawson Turner, 'for a man of my high reputation to make humanity the subject of private speculation?' Dawson Turner did not commit himself on this point, but gave his opinion, as a practical banker, that the financial state of the country was unfavourable to such a venture.

For the time, Manby resisted the blandishments of commerce, and continued to pin his hopes upon Parliament. Meanwhile, Lord Russell had raised the question of Criminal Reform in the House, and Manby saw in this a chance to resurrect his plans for a convict colony in Greenland. He wrote to Russell, enclosing copies of the letters he had formerly written to Lord Grey on the same subject. Russell, through his secretary, actually replied: he said 'it would have his deepest consideration'.[3] Manby was desperately anxious to contact Buckingham, so that he could advise in the drafting of the Shipwreck Bill; but Buckingham had gone to ground. 'I wrote and offered my assistance,' Manby told Dawson Turner. 'The answer—a letter of humbug.'

Manby's month ran out, and so did his money, and the only tangible result was a greatly increased load of debt. The bill for printing and engraving alone—nearly double the original estimate —was terrifying to think about. There was no doubt in his mind that once the prints started to sell, the expense would be more than justified; he was confident, too, that there would be a big demand for his pamphlet once Buckingham's Bill came before the House. Unfortunately, the Bill had been delayed because of pressure of other business.

With so many irons in the fire about to reach white heat, it was imperative for him to remain in London. It was unthinkable to give up now for the want of a few pounds. He wrote to Dawson Turner, dispatching his letter by carriage—the most expensive means available. Once, many years before, Turner had unwisely told Manby that he would always be pleased to pay postage on his letters. 'You did not mention conveyance by carriage,' Manby wrote, 'however, I hope your generosity extends to the latter, as I avail myself of it.' The remainder of the letter was only too familiar. He asked a favour—perhaps the last favour he would ever ask—a loan of £5. 'I pledge my honour I will pay it back when I draw my pay at the end of the month. It will save my medals.'

Dawson Turner sent the money, with a curt note telling Manby he must return to Yarmouth immediately Buckingham's Bill had been read. Manby took this to imply the banker's approval.

'I know your explicitness proceeds from the kindest feelings,' he wrote back. 'I shall take your advice and stay in Town until Buckingham's Bill is disposed of. My only regret is on account of my wife. You will therefore, at your most convenient leisure, oblige me by seeing her and stating it is by your advice. Most certainly at the present moment, it is most necessary that such advice should be taken, for never was a more propitious moment for reaching the object I have had so many years at heart. It is intensely cold. To-morrow I meet the Committee of the Zoological Society to inspect the bones of a whale.'

When Buckingham's Bill was published, it became clear why its author had been so carefully avoiding Manby. The saving of life from shipwreck was scarcely mentioned, and there was no suggestion of a special department for this purpose. It was a staggering blow, and the effect of so much punishment was beginning to tell. The balance of his mind, always precarious since the operation on his head, could no longer withstand such shocks. The blinding headaches became more frequent; his behaviour more peculiar; his memory played tricks, and there were times when past, present and future became confused, and the distinction between fact and fantasy blurred. He would not, could not give up; but now he was like a marksman who had expended all his genuine ammunition without effect, who could no longer see the target, but who continued to fling wildly any object he could lay his hands upon in the hope of hitting something . . . *anything*.

In his Adelphi chambers, the rent of which had not been paid for he could not remember how long, he sat surrounded by mountains of unsold pamphlets and prints, writing a frenzied spate of petitions, addresses, memorials, statements of services, appeals and grand designs to Palmerston, Peel, Russell and Melbourne. Sometimes he worked all night, until he collapsed with exhaustion. And yet, amid all this insane turmoil, a part of his mind remained remote, and functioned with a lucid brilliance, planning the first steam-powered lifeboat.

His disappointment with Buckingham's Bill made it seem more important than ever to stay in London, despite the letters he had been receiving from the Barrack Sergeant, couched in stately non-commissioned language, begging to inform him that Mrs Manby was ill; and others from Frost, timidly reproachful, that she was in a state of penury. He asked Dawson Turner to investigate, adding: 'I will throw over the grand objects I am labouring for, and come at a summons—but I hope it will not be necessary.'

In June, the summons came, but from another quarter. The Barrack Board ordered him to return immediately to his duties. The King, who had been ill for some time, was now on the point of death. Although it was not expected that his demise would result in the joyous riots that had followed the death of his brother, nevertheless, it was necessary for the Military to be in a state of preparation, if only for solemn parades.

'My presence at the Barracks is indispensable,' he wrote to Dawson Turner, 'and unfortunately puts me to the expense of travel. Oblige me by telling Mrs Manby I shall come to Yarmouth on the *Enterprise* on Tuesday night.'

The King died, and Victoria came to the throne, on June 20th. William might have been the best of a sorry procession of reprobates and idiots who had ruled England for a hundred years; but there were few who felt much grief at his passing. Least of all Manby, whom he had slighted and ignored, setting a Royal example of prejudice which had percolated down through all ranks of the administration.

The Victorian era opened for Manby with soaring hopes. At last, it seemed, there was a monarch favourably disposed towards him, who he was sure would be quick to right the wrongs he had suffered at the hands of her relatives. He could congratulate himself on his perspicacity in cultivating the Duchess of Kent, and there was the comforting memory of that wonderful moment on the Isle of Wight when Victoria had pressed his book to her bosom and promised to get it by heart. The shadowy knighthood he had chased so long seemed suddenly once again within his grasp.

William the Fourth had scarcely breathed his last before Manby was writing to the Duchess of Kent, requesting her to place his prints at Her Majesty's feet. 'I rejoice to see in the papers,' he told Dawson Turner, who helped him write the application, 'the warm interest the Queen takes in the Navy. Recollecting what happened in the Isle of Wight, I believe my prints will receive a Royal welcome.' The Duchess replied, through Conroy, that the matter could not be pursued until after the late King's funeral.

Of more immediate importance than his knighthood, was his need for money. He submitted to the Admiralty a Memorial asking for compensation for the expenses he had incurred for his life-saving apparatus. The reply, for the Admiralty, was extremely prompt: 'I am commanded by their Lordships to acquaint you that My Lords regret that they cannot interfere.' Mr Young advised him to petition Parliament, and promised to use his influence with Lord Melbourne. 'I shall ask as little as possible,' Manby told Dawson Turner, 'to prevent refusal—only what will free me from my present embarrassments.'

Meanwhile, a faint gleam of encouragement emanated from the obscurity of the Colonial Office. A letter told him that 'the question of establishing your apparatus for preserving lives from shipwreck in the Colonies is proceeding. Many parties must be consulted, and considerable delay elapse, before Lord Glenelg[4] will arrive at a decision on the subject.'

In the autumn, a distracted letter arrived from France. It was from Georgina. The gloomy predictions of disaster that had preceded the wedding had proved to be correct. Manby could not fully understand the details from his niece's wild letter; but it was clear Sir Cavendish was in serious trouble. He had disappeared. The British authorities had declared him an outlaw, and he was wanted by the French police. Georgina was staying with the Barronne de Feuchères, but she intended to come to London to seek Manby's help as her guardian and trustee.

It was February the following year before Manby was able to

get back to London. His mind, he said, had been sinking into a state of imbecility in Yarmouth, but once back in the hub of things, it was restored to a degree of energy to excite astonishment at so great a change. He stayed at the York Hotel. Before leaving London in June, he had written to his landlord, giving up the tenancy of the Adelphi rooms. At least, he thought he had written. There had, admittedly, been no reply from Mr Allenby, but since Manby owed six months rent, he did not concern himself unduly about this. He had left at the chambers, to collect at a convenient time, a number of cases containing his papers, models and bulky lithographic stones. He had also left his medals. Manby was quite content for the papers, models and stones to be stored at Allenby's expense while he found new lodgings; but he was anxious to regain possession of his medals at the earliest possible moment. He was lonely and unhappy without his medals; he longed to see their friendly gold and silver faces, and feel their comforting weight in his hands. Besides, he was sure they would soon be urgently required to wear on some very important occasion—perhaps even to show a most illustrious person.

When Manby called at number 13 Adelphi, he found his way barred by a formidable housekeeper. No, he could not go up to his old rooms—Mr Allenby had given strict instructions. In any event, his property was no longer there, Mr Allenby had removed it. She did not know where. Mr Allenby himself was not available; she believed he was at Kingston.[5]

Outraged, Manby took a cab to Lincoln's Inn, intent on immediate legal action. His lawyer, however, was out, and his anger began to give place to a dreadful sense of fear. Suppose Allenby had disposed of the medals to defray the arrears of rent? He might even have a legal right to do so. The possibility was too terrible to think about, and in an effort to force it from his mind, he went to St James's Park where a large number of people were skating on the ice-covered lake. It was some consolation to see that his rescue apparatus was on hand ready for use. He sought out the

Park Superintendent, who told him that there had been thirty-three rescues that winter, twenty-nine lives had been saved, and four had been lost. Manby asked him to furnish a written certificate to this effect, and then caused a minor sensation by having himself punted out to the centre of the ice, sitting on one of the wicker sledges he had invented in 1814.

Two days later, a letter came from Allenby. 'The time has arrived,' the landlord wrote, 'to speak plainly. I have this-morning received notice from home that you called for your medals. As you know, you took the rooms for a year. You must also know that your rent is now overdue—you gave me no notice of your intention to give them up last May. I have never concealed from you that I am a poor man, struggling with adversity. The want of money forced me to place the medals in the hands of Charles Harrison, Esq., 14 Southampton Buildings, Charing Cross, to whom I refer you for the settlement of the matter.'[6]

With this letter was a bill for £61, the amount of rent outstanding to the end of January. Manby was panic-stricken, and sent out a frantic appeal to Dawson Turner.

'Need I be under any apprehension of Allenby or Harrison arresting me?' he wrote. 'If so, for God's sake inform me how I can raise the money. Permit me to ask, as a matter of business, is there any means to raise money on the annuity due in four months? I must have my medals; Mr Young touched upon honours from foreign sovereigns in his letter to Lord Melbourne, and I need them to show Conroy to induce him to get an interview with the Duchess of Kent, to exhibit to her. I told Allenby I was leaving in June, and requested him to let the rooms. He has probably had the rent since June, but how can I prove it?'

While he waited anxiously for Dawson Turner's verdict, he once again called at the Adelphi. He was determined to brave the female dragon and find out for certain if Allenby was double-crossing him, and had, in fact, been letting the rooms to another tenant. This time there was no one at home but a simple, garrulous housemaid, who told him innocently that the rooms had been let to a Mr Pearce. Manby and the maid were caught red-handed by the returning housekeeper. The maid was dismissed in tears under threats of dire punishment, while Manby, after a heated and undignified altercation, found himself back on the pavement with the door of Number 13 firmly slammed in his face.

Dawson Turner did not send Manby the money; but he did pay the £61 direct to Allenby's lawyer. The medals were saved. It had been a nasty moment; but now that it was over, Manby's self-centred confidence bounced back unimpaired, and he contrived to make it appear that he was the injured party. The severe letter Turner wrote, telling him he would do better to think more of his wife, and less of his medals, hardly touched him.

'I was sorry,' he wrote back, 'to observe in your last letter almost a reprimand for not supplying Mrs Manby with her wants. I left money with Frost—Mrs Manby preferred this—and I distinctly asked her before leaving if there was anything she wanted.' What more, he implied, could any husband have done? He himself, after all, was deserving of sympathy. The recent anxiety over his medals had affected his health. 'I now find it necessary to live better,' he pointed out, 'and to take wine to support my strength, which old age is fast taking.'

He needed all his strength, for there was so much to do. Georgina had arrived in London with the Barronne. The Barronne was ill, and Georgina in a state of hysterical distress. 'She wished to beggar herself,' Manby wrote, 'to assist her husband; but as her trustee, I refused to allow this for so worthless and undeserving a man.'

Everything was suddenly happening at once. Lord Glenelg summoned him for a most flattering interview. 'I left him with a well-arranged plan for being appointed to perfect a most important service,' Manby wrote, 'and I expect 'ere the week closes to hear something very satisfactory.' He had also seen Conroy, who had told him that he had no doubt Lord Melbourne would urge upon the Queen the vital importance of Manby's services, and that a fair pension, if nothing else, would be granted. 'I left my publication on saving from ice,' he said, 'and asked if it would be acceptable to the Duchess of Kent. He said he was sure—greatest of pleasure—and would take it himself that afternoon, if possible, to the parlour.'

Lord Russell had not been able to see Manby personally about the Greenland project—pressure of business was too great—but he had asked for details to be put in writing. 'I spent all morning (suitable because of snow) doing this. I will send you a copy of the letter, which may hereafter be an interesting and highly important document.'

Things were moving, too, in another direction. He was to be presented by the doubtfully Royal Society for the Preservation of Life from Fire with a medal for his invention of a jumping sheet, designed to break the fall of persons jumping from the upper windows of houses in flames. He understood the medal was to be distinguished from all others, even the one presented to the Queen.

There seemed no doubt that the tide was now flowing in his favour, but there was no softening of his brother-in-law's vicious vendetta. Manby was worried that the cruel injustice of the baronet's calumnies would ruin his chance of recognition by the new Queen. 'The Duke of Sussex[7] now ignores me,' he told Dawson Turner, 'and I fear he may influence the Duchess of Kent against me. I did nothing to deserve this pertinacious victimization.'

The day he wrote this letter was the twentieth anniversary of his marriage to Sophia. He added a footnote: 'If you see my wife, give her my affectionate love, and tell her I will drink her health. Will you also quieten her mind by telling her how advantageous it is for me to stay in London?'

The ice melted on the lake in St James's Park, and Manby's wicker sledge, the ladders and the grappling poles were put away until next winter. Now that there was no ice to fall through, the citizens of London looked around for an alternative means of self-destruction. One, a boy of fourteen, found an original method provided by the Society for the Preservation of Life from Fire. The Society had sponsored a competition for life-saving devices, and the first prize had gone to the inventor of a portable fire-escape. The escape was to have a public demonstration one Saturday afternoon, and been installed in the grounds of Charing Cross Barracks. An hour before the show was due to start, the boy decided to try the apparatus out for himself. 'He attempted,' Manby wrote, 'to escape from a lofty window. Fear disengaged him from the apparatus and he fell and was killed.'

It was a tragedy that did not inspire confidence in the new method of escape; but for Manby it had its brighter side, and brought him some useful publicity. 'I attended the inquest,' he told Dawson Turner. 'Accidental death. I was treated with such attention by the Coroner, that I availed myself of the opportunity to make some remarks on the cause of destructive fires, with suggestions for diminishing loss of life and property by that calamity in the Metropolis.' It was gratifying to think that the child had not died in vain. 'We often look on occurrences in reference to the pain they give us at the time,' he explained sententiously, 'without waiting to rejoice if such partial evil may not tend to some important good.'

He had planned to return to Yarmouth at the end of the month; but at the last moment he was summoned to the Treasury. He was seen by an under-secretary, who told him the incredible news that the government had decided to grant his petition for compensation. Unfortunately Mr Baring, who had taken charge of the papers, was unexpectedly away owing to the sudden death of his wife. However, Manby could expect the money within a few days. There was no mention of the exact amount of the grant; but really, the amount was unimportant beside the glorious fact that at last a shadow had taken on solid substance, and his great services to humanity were being officially recognised. It was the first step, and the day when he would be addressed as Sir George, so long awaited, now seemed very close. He wrote happily to Dawson Turner, to explain why he was staying in London after all. 'If you should see Mrs Manby,' he said, 'emphasise the reason for my detention in Town, for should it get to the ears of her family, they will say I dare not return to Yarmouth.'

12

THE CHEQUE ON Coutts' Bank which Manby received from the Treasury was for £600. It was a niggardly sum, and worked out at less than one pound for every life Manby had been the means of saving. Nevertheless, it did suffice to free him from his present embarrassments, which was what he had asked for. To Manby, although his hopes had been floating in the thousands, the precise amount was of less importance than the fact that he had at last broken through the barrier of official indifference. He looked upon the £600 as a first instalment.

'Thank God I am at last out of debt,' he wrote to Dawson Turner. 'I had the delight to-day of paying £500 into Barclay's for transmission to your Bank. I retained £100 to pay various long bills in Town. I must now endeavour to advance myself in connection with the Coronation. I have sent a Memorial to Lord Melbourne in respect of pensions granted to inventors for the preservation of life, and I will attend the Master General's levee on Saturday to keep the thought alive.'

Manby had no idea how much money he really owed, or the speed with which his creditors would pounce on his £600. He was happy in his ignorance, enjoying enormously an illusion of wealth. He mellowed, and now that he could afford it, he did his best to relieve his wife's miserable existence. It was late in the day —too late—but he did try. He looked around for suitable lodgings so that Sophia and Frost could join him in London, and fixed on a boarding house near Charing Cross. The house was in Warwick Square, a quiet, pleasant situation, opposite a statue of George the Third. Manby dined there and found the fare excellent and liberal, while the terms were remarkably moderate—two guineas a week for Mrs Manby, and fifteen shillings for Frost.

'I have engaged the most delightful appartments for Mrs Manby,' he told Dawson Turner, 'where there is society which at meals and in the drawing room will render it delightful to her. As there is no accommodation for self, books, papers, etc., I have taken a room in the house next door—this will also prevent interruption when deeply employed. I will take meals with my wife, and, when daily studies over, I shall be ready and happy to attend to her amusement.'

He left it to the Barrack Sergeant to arrange, and Dawson Turner to finance, the journey. The two ladies were to travel by steamer; Manby would meet them with a coach and conduct them to their new abode. He never doubted that Sophia would be overcome with gratitude at the plans he was making on her behalf. It did not occur to him to question whether two elderly, frail and simple women, who had lived so long in seclusion, wished to be abruptly uprooted from their familiar surroundings, and dumped among strangers in the middle of a frightening and unfriendly city.

For a time, all was idyllic. 'It is impossible to express Mrs Manby's delight at my having provided for her such a delightful situation,' he wrote enthusiastically to Dawson Turner. 'I walk with her every day, and show her something new to amuse. We

have just returned from the Geological Museum, and paying my
York Hotel bill. I am getting Mrs Manby everything she requires,
and Frost everything she could wish for.' A few days later, he
reported a visit to the Colosseum and the Botanical Gardens. 'It
was delightful to see how much she enjoyed,' he wrote, 'her joy
at feeding the monkeys was like a child.'

But the novelty soon wore thin, and Manby's good intentions
flagged. He found himself becoming bored and restless, and the
after-dinner sessions in the boarding house parlour grew intoler-
able. As for Sophia, the delights of fossils and monkeys soon palled.
She longed to be back in her own home, among her own posses-
sions.

Frost, too, was miserable; utterly out of her element. London
terrified her, she was confused and intimidated, constantly on the
verge of tears. 'Poor Frost seems far from well,' Manby told
Dawson Turner.

Frost's health was an excuse all parties fixed upon eagerly. At
the end of the month, the two women went back to Yarmouth,
and the sheltered obscurity of the Barracks. After a London
boarding house, even the loneliness was a pleasure. It was a relief,
too, for Manby to see them go. He was satisfied that he had done
his best, and that the accusations of neglect by his wife's relatives
had been effectively silenced. Now, unhampered and with a clear
conscience, he could concentrate on pressing home his sudden
change of fortune.

'The sun of good fortune appears every day, and brightly
shines upon me,' he wrote to Dawson Turner. 'The best and most
cutting reproof to those low, grovelling and contemptible minds
who have attempted to blight my reputation and dishonour my
name. I will not exult on success, but treat their despicable conduct with contempt.'

His one anxiety was whether his health would give way at this
crucial moment in his career. 'Although my mind is now at rest,'
he wrote, 'the excitement and apprehension of the last few years

have played havoc with my constitution. I have nearly lost the use
of my left hand through the contraction of the fingers.'

To Manby, because it was his own hand, this condition was
unique and remarkable. As with his head, he felt his hand should
be preserved. 'I wish to ask your advice about the amputation of
hand as well as head at death,' he told Dawson Turner. 'I wish to
confer with you on this subject of such importance to science.'

Manby's high-minded attitude towards making humanity the
subject of private speculation had been weakened by the unsatisfactory nature of Buckingham's Bill. It was undermined still
further when, after continual delays, it seemed unlikely that the
Bill, however disappointing, would ever reach the Statute Book.
At long last, the futility of relying on purely governmental action
was coming home to him. What appeared to succeed was private
enterprise working with Parliamentary blessing and government
protection. The railways, which were being built all over the
country, provided a striking example. Private enterprise provided
the capital and got on with the job; the government awarded
monopolies and gave legal sanctions.

When Mr Young and his business confrères approached Manby
with the proposal of forming a company to exploit his scheme for
raising sunken property, he fell an easy victim, especially as he
was to be appointed a director and presented with a block of
shares. The company was to be called The Submarine and Wreck
Weighing Association, and its declared object was the recovering
of cargoes and hulls, and for preserving the lives of crews and ships
in distress. Captain John Ross,[1] the Arctic explorer whom Manby
greatly admired, and the Hon. Arthur Dumcombe M.P., were
also to be on the board, their names lending an air of respectability
to what was, in effect, a bucket-shop operation.

An impressive prospectus was drawn up, inviting the public to
invest in the new company. The aim was to raise £250,000 by
selling 10,000 £25 shares. Investors were given the promise of a

return of at least 25 per cent, and assured that an Act of Parliament would give the company a monopoly of raising sunken property. Twenty-six stations were to be established around the coast, in charge of Naval lieutenants, with schooners, salvage machinery and diving equipment. The outlay on each station was estimated at £3,000, they would cost £1,000 a year to maintain, and produce an income of £83,000. The total yearly income of the company, according to these sanguine calculations would be over two million pounds.[2]

Manby, and possibly his fellow directors, were as much the victims of this fiction as the country parsons, the small shopkeepers and the widowed ladies who parted with their savings. Manby proudly sent Dawson Turner a draft copy of the prospectus, and was genuinely astonished at the violence of the banker's reaction. Dawson Turner did not hesitate to say that, in his opinion, the whole thing was a fraud. It was criminally misleading to say that the company was to be incorporated by an Act of Parliament; there was no such Act and the possibility of there ever being one was negligible. As for the estimates of costs and profits, these were pure imagination, designed deliberately to appeal to the greed and gullibility of the public. He advised Manby to dissociate himself immediately from a project so patently dishonest.

Manby took no notice. The idea of wealth had now taken a powerful hold on his mind. He would not only be Sir George William Manby, he would be rich Sir George William Manby. The dream, for him, was the reality, and although he was hurt by his friend's harsh, censorious attitude, he excused and dismissed it as a manifestation of the banker's conventional, provincial mind and excessive caution. Manby was prepared to ignore completely Turner's opposition to the Wreck Weighing Association; but for Turner, it was the end. Over the years it had become increasingly evident that Manby was a liar, a man who could not be trusted in matters of money, who was selfish to a pathological degree, and

Gold medal from King Charles X of France

Queen Victoria's Coronation Medal

Manby's monument

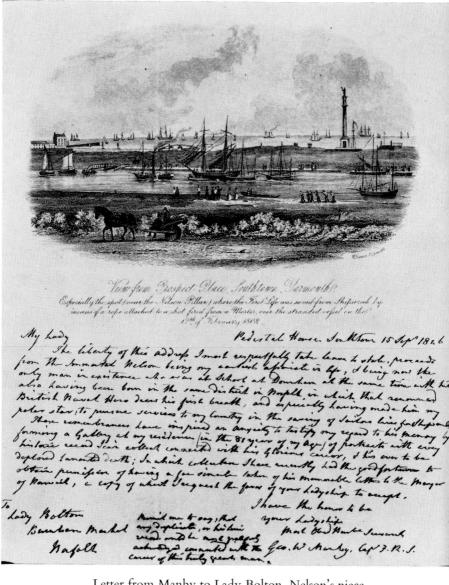

View from Prospect Place, Southtown, Yarmouth.
Especially the spot (near the Nelson Pillar) where the First Life was saved from Shipwreck by
means of a rope attached to a shot fired from a Mortar, over the stranded vessel on the
12th of February, 1808.

Letter from Manby to Lady Bolton, Nelson's niece

whose motives, even for his most altruistic seeming schemes, were always suspect. But, although each new revelation of the flaws in Manby's character had been a painful process of disillusionment, the banker had been able to stretch and adjust his moral code to accommodate them. The man, after all, was a genius, to whom normal standards did not apply; underlying everything, however outrageous, was a genuine and extraordinary desire to benefit humanity; he had been the means of saving thousands of lives, and his faults, however deplorable, were innocent, in the sense that they were part of his personality. They were not deliberate or premeditated, and Manby himself did not know they existed. When it came to business, however, the banker's code was inflexible. The foundation of his world was commercial integrity; without it the whole structure of an ordered system collapsed in chaos; it must be preserved and protected at all costs; friendship, even love, must take second place. He did not entirely sever all connections with Manby but the dearest friend of his earlier letters, became curtly 'Sir'.

Manby did not seem to notice; the flow of his confidences and his demands continued uninhibited. There was so much to tell; he was involved in so many momentous events, the possibility that Turner no longer wished to hear about them was something it took a long time for him to realise. It was the telling which was important; the listener's reaction hardly concerned him. Someone *must* listen, and there was no one else.

Another venture in which the public were invited to buy shares at this time was the Polytechnic Institute shortly to be opened in Regent Street. The Polytechnic aimed to encourage practical science and provide a permanent exhibition where inventors and manufacturers could display and demonstrate their latest machines and processes.[3] The income was to derive from renting space and from admission fees. Manby saw in the Polytechnic a great opportunity for advertising himself and his inventions. He also saw the chance of gaining kudos by insinuating himself as one of the founders. 'My time and thought,' he wrote, 'is occupied in associating my name with the origin of the Institute.' There was not much left of his £600, but he managed to buy £100 of shares. 'They only dispose of Poly Shares to distinguished persons,' he told Turner. 'I received mine without premium, although £15 has been offered.' The directors, he said, had allocated him a specially favourable position where he intended to hold an exhibition of his models, with his medals in a glass case, and pictures by the brothers Joy depicting rescues at sea on either side. His pamphlets and prints would be on sale, and he was sure that when the Poly opened in August, demand would be enormous.

At the end of June, Victoria was crowned Queen of England. Manby was awoken on the great morning by the noises of axes and hammers of the workmen putting the finishing touches to the public stands. Immediately the Queen had been officially anointed, Manby submitted a statement of his services, adding his hope that Her Majesty would wish to reward in a fitting manner a man who had devoted himself to saving so many of her subjects' valuable lives. The reply was as prompt as it was brief: 'Lord J. Russell begs to inform you that he has laid before the Queen your application for Her Majesty's bounty. He regrets there are no funds which would enable Her Majesty to comply with your suggestion.'[4]

Undeterred by this rebuff, Manby went ahead with his plans to dedicate to the Queen an Address to the British Public on which he had been working and which was to be the first piece of printing to come off a powerful steam operated press on display at the Polytechnic. The Address was a summary of his life-saving efforts, with remarks on the raising of sunken property designed to advertise the new Submarine and Wreck Weighing Company. In the face of Dawson Turner's views on this subject, Manby had the temerity to send him a copy with the request that he write the dedication. 'Please favour with suitable dedication to Queen,' he wrote, 'as encourager of science—warm friend of humanity. Following work—result of labour of life spent in devising methods of preservation of H.M.'s subjects. Excellent opportunity to touch on late Duke of Kent's memorable advice at my first public experiment in Hyde Park. If you would incorporate this subject and send to me by Sat. post, I would transcribe and send to Poly directors. Will have happy effect, and improve my position with the Institute and with H.M.'[5]

Turner did not compose the dedication; but he wrote to say that Manby's wife was seriously ill. 'If Mrs Manby's health deteriorates, write again,' Manby replied, 'and I will return. I have asked the Barrack Sergeant to report every day, and Frost is present. I must stay in Town if possible, for today is the rehearsal of all Poly exhibitioners. It is an honour to our country—no one to more advantage than self.'

While he was frantically busy preparing for the opening of the Polytechnic, Manby was the victim of yet another accident. This time, walking through Covent Garden, he was hit on the leg by the lid of a basket thrown by a porter. His injuries provided him with a further excuse for staying in London, despite the increasingly alarming reports on Sophia's health which were reaching him from Yarmouth. 'The contents of your last letter was not pleasing,' he wrote to Turner. 'But I have great confidence in Doctor Cox and your great interest in Mrs Manby. When she desires to see me I will forgo every circumstance however important to my advancement to comply with such request. This is my first duty. I fear, however, my leg is still painful. I am unable to walk and cannot afford cabs.'

Neither his leg nor his lack of cash prevented him from attending the private view of the Polytechnic at the beginning of August. One thousand tickets had been distributed; representatives of the press were there in force, including Mr Bell Stephens, the Editor of the *Morning Post*. Mr Stephens took a flattering interest in Manby's display, and in his report next day he singled out Manby for particular notice. Generally his remarks on the Polytechnic were sardonic. He was not impressed with the apparatus which cooked a mutton shop at a distance of 110 feet; he poked fun at the diving bell in which five persons could descend to the bottom of a large tank of water; but 'the unrequited inventions of Captain Manby, clearly and beautifully illustrated by the author with models and drawings,' he found by far the most interesting and important to humanity.

'Shipwrecked sailors appeal to British feeling with a force one would think irresistible,' he wrote. 'Captain Manby alone has fully responded to this appeal, and now the extensive museum of his maritime inventions form a cabinet whose merit is gratefully acknowledged by every sailor; of admiration and public honours abroad; of undisputed efficiency and extensive application—and no rewards or honours at home. We fearlessly predict, however, that its daily exhibition will accumulate such a mass of public opinion in favour of the long deserving inventor that those "clothed in a little brief authority" will not long attempt to resist his well-founded claims for public consideration and natural gratitude.'

'Now, maybe, I will get recognition,' Manby wrote, sending Turner a cutting of this paragraph. 'I shall call on Mr Stephens to acknowledge his flattering notice.'

On the day this report was published, Manby received a letter from Yarmouth, enclosing one from Doctor Cox. 'I do not think it likely Mrs Manby will survive many days,' he read. 'Will you communicate with Captain Manby. Breathing worse, and if chest gets worse she will immediately sink.'

Still he did not return home. He was ready, he said, to leave at a moment's notice; but it was so important now that his name was rising in popular estimation to be on the spot. He had arranged, in any event, to descend in the new diving bell, which he believed would be of great value in the raising of sunken property. He was also deeply engaged on a new scheme to protect the mouth of the river Yare and to prevent ships reaching the town in the event of an invasion. 'My poor brain has no rest,' he wrote. 'The material for the boom must be of a quality to hinder, indestructible by enemy, and to be simply stretched across the river when required. I have a man at work on a model[6] and on Saturday next intend to place it in the Poly and to submit it to the Government. By the end of the week, my work will be done. Indeed, I am indefatigable and if I do not die affluent, I will obtain what is due to me—*Fame.*'

Sophia, defying Doctor Cox's gloomy prognosis, made a miraculous recovery. She was confined to a wheel chair; but by the end of the year the danger, for the time being, was definitely over. Christmas 1838, however, was not a joyous one for Manby. His infatuation with the Polytechnic had turned sour. One of the directors had raised outspoken objections to the way in which Manby was using the Institute to publicise, and lend an air of respectability to, the dubious Submarine and Wreck Weighing Association. This was particularly unfortunate at a moment when gracious permission had just been granted to dedicate his Address to the Queen.

'My feelings on the Poly you know,' he wrote to Dawson Turner, full of righteous indignation. 'I viewed all the directors as honourable—except one who is presumptuous and browbeating and disgusts me. His conduct had been so highly objectionable I considered it necessary to withdraw further arrangements for bringing to practice services of highest importance to the nation—for recovering sunken property and raising vessels. My eyes have been opened and I now view the proceedings of the Institute in a different light. The person is a notorious intriguer and I intend to instigate an inquiry into the management of the Institute.'

Dawson Turner's reply was unsympathetic. Once again he advised Manby to dissociate himself from the Submarine and Wreck Raising Association.

'Your letter seriously affected my spirits,' Manby wrote back, 'and brought on a distressing debility and nervous cough. I have made up my mind to dispose of my Poly shares, sell my works for whatever they will fetch, return home and never undertake anything again. I shall spend the remainder of my days in quiet and not subject myself to have my temper tortured ever again by demands.'

13

FOR A TIME IT seemed Manby was serious in his resolve to give up the struggle and retire into senile obscurity. He withdrew to the Barracks: he sold his Polytechnic shares; he resigned his directorship of the Submarine and Wreck Weighing Association; he gave his models and his drawings to the Norwich Museum. He discarded everything except hope. The mirage of a knighthood continued to shimmer before his eyes, and when, at the end of 1841, Prince Edward was born, the illusion took on a renewed brilliance.

The arrival of an heir was celebrated by a surge of Royal generosity. The accolade was falling freely on the shoulders of men whose merits were obviously inferior to his own. There had never been a time, he felt convinced, more favourable for attaining his great ambition. He wrote a series of letters to Peel, stating his claims and, when these were not answered, he petitioned the Queen directly.

The Queen responded. In March, 1842, a communication from St James's Palace arrived at the Barracks. The appearance of the packet was promising; it was heavy and impressive; it left little doubt in Manby's mind that here, at last, was his knighthood. Trembling with joyful expectation, he opened the envelope and read the Royal letter.

'Sir Henry Wheatley presents his compliments to Capt. Manby, and is honoured with the Queen's Commands to beg his acceptance of the accompanying Gold Coronation Medal, as a small mark of the sense Her Majesty entertains of the usefulness of his inventions in the Preservation of Lives from Shipwreck.

'Sir Henry has further to inform Capt. Manby that all applications for Marks of Royal favour and distinction for services rendered to the State must be submitted and recommended to Her Majesty by the Prime Minister.'[1]

Manby was accustomed to disappointment; he was hardened to the blows of fate; but this was the cruellest stroke of all, and it shattered him completely. The Coronation Medal! The sort of award handed out to stationmasters and time-serving civil servants—and sent through the post like a tradesman's sample. Victoria's insulting minor honour was worse than the neglect of George the Third, the active malice of George the Fourth or the broken promises of William.

It was incredible, and Manby refused to believe that a lifetime of high endeavour could end in this paltry way. He read and re-read the letter, seeking some clue to the mystery; some faint gleam of encouragement. He fixed upon the final paragraph, seeing in it what he desperately desired to see—an invitation to apply for further honours. A more probable interpretation was that the Queen did not desire any further solicitations from Captain Manby, and the medal was the utmost he could expect. Manby, however, decided that the paragraph was 'one of those noble hints so peculiar to Her Majesty's great mind'.[2] It was as though the beautiful young woman with the penetrating eyes, who had pressed his essays to her bosom, was whispering confidentially that because of all the tiresome red tape surrounding these things, stuffy old Sir Robert would have to be brought in—simply as a formality.

The power of self-delusion triumphed over reason and experience. Once again he wrote to Peel. He was doing so, he said, because of the unsolicited suggestion made to him by command of Her Majesty. 'Under the influence of such suggestion, and from a desire to stimulate others to pursue a path worthy of British followers by an enthusiastic devotedness to Loyalty, Patriotism and Benevolence, I humbly presume to lay before you as a faithful record, a detailed statement of the Services I have rendered, leaving it to your influential position to decide whether they are of sufficient import to make me worthy of recommendation to a noble-minded sovereign.'[3]

It was a long letter; it took several weeks to write. In it he summarised his humanitarian activities, starting in 1793 when he had rescued a soldier from a burning tent, and ending with the thousand sailors who had been saved by his apparatus—eighty of that number by his own hand, and some at great risk to his own life in the undertaking. 'I was the first human being that ever projected a rope from a piece of ordnance, for the preservation of my fellow men, and devised the method of bearing them safely to the shore. From the time when the idea occurred to me, I determined to carry it into effect, and I have unflinchingly worked my way through good report and evil report, 'till I have had the unspeakable satisfaction of seeing the system adopted on the shore of every maritime nation in Europe, stamped with my name.'

Peel wavered; perhaps, after all, this man *was* worth more than a Coronation Medal. He decided to refer the letter to his close friend and political supporter, Sir James Graham, asking for his opinion.

'When I was at the Admiralty,' Graham replied, 'I received numerous applications from Capt. Manby, and the late King was tormented by his importunity. He was a great friend of the late Queen Caroline, and he is a man of whom I formed no very favourable opinion. His reward has been so long postponed, it may stand over for the present without any great injustice.'⁴

Manby was never to know that the last chance of the honour he craved was lost because Graham made the incredible blunder of confusing him with his brother Thomas. It never occurred to him that Graham, who had paid him so many after-dinner compliments, was unable to distinguish between the living Captain Manby, and a man, dead now for years, who once in his youth had been involved in a Royal scandal. He was to die ignorant of the cruel twist of fate that had made him responsible for his brother's sins, as well as his own.

Peel, or someone on his staff, might have checked the facts; but no one troubled, and Peel, horrified how close he had come to recommending to Victoria a man of such unsavoury reputation, hurriedly drafted his refusal on the back of Graham's letter.

'Although I do not think it advisable to recommend to Her Majesty a compliance with this application, I assure you that my decision rests upon general considerations, and is not influenced by any disposition to underrate the services to which your letter refers.' He added: 'or to call into question the disinterestedness of your motives', but, on second thoughts, crossed this out.⁵

Manby was completely baffled. If the Prime Minister did not underrate his services, what, then, did he mean by 'general considerations'? He felt convinced there had been some misunderstanding, and wrote back to say that he feared he had not made himself understood in his application. Both the Queen and her Royal Father had already acknowledged the value of his services; 'but these distinctions, however flattering, are comparatively known to few, and I am most anxious to place these services upon record after I am dead'. He was entitled, he felt, to be placed among the Companions of the Honourable Order of the Bath, but failing this 'I should be most thankful for a knighthood'.

This time there was no personal reply from Peel, only a brief note from a secretary: 'Sir R. Peel does not feel himself enabled to comply with your request.'[6]

'I have too high a mind to repeat my application,' Manby wrote.[7] 'But I have carefully reviewed the occurrences of my life, and find nothing that I wish to have done otherwise. Benevolence I have exercised to the utmost of my power, and a devotedness to humanity has been the guide of my conduct. There is no one action of my long life upon which I look back with regret. How often those who endeavour to attain public distinction by their labours, meet with the pestilent and vulgar propensity of envy, or prejudice, and when the baneful influence of the latter emanates from those in the higher walks of life, the poison can be diffused stealthily, and the victim shut out of Society, by unmerited persecution, by fabrication of the grossest falsehoods, promulgated with the basest wickedness and most infamous intentness to destroy his character. This is a subject which has given me the greatest pain, and would have rendered life scarcely desirable or even supportable, was it not from the fullest reliance on Religion, and its support in the moment of heaviest affliction.'

Manby had lived too long; he was a trespasser in Victorian England presided over by Sir Robert Peel. In an age of steam and electricity, the professionals with their slide rules were taking over. The dilettanti and the amateurs were being shouldered out. In other ways, too, Manby had become an anachronism. Although sinecures and multiple offices still flourished, the tide of Reform was lapping at the fringes of the system, and it was the little men with their minor privileges who were the first to be washed away. Manby was nearly eighty; he had been Master of the Yarmouth Barracks and receiving public money for nominal duties for forty years. He had come to look upon the position and the salary as his personal property for life.

Manby was still reeling form the blows he had received from the Queen and Peel, when the Barrack Board followed up with a *coup de grâce.* They wrote curtly to say that they were terminating his appointment, and directed him to leave the Barracks at the earliest possible moment, since his residence was required for the new Master. 'This, after forty years devoted service to the Department,' Manby wrote distractedly to Dawson Turner. 'The moment is fraught with danger. For God's sake can you help?'

Dawson Turner did nothing; there was, perhaps, nothing he could do. In any event he, too, was an old man occupied with the self-centred problems of senescence. Manby's continuing demands were an embarrassing echo from the past, like the importunities of a long discarded mistress. Manby's own desperate appeals to the Board met with an equally unsympathetic response. He wrote imploring a few months' grace on account of his wife's delicate state of health. The Board replied: 'We trust Mrs Manby will experience no ill effect in removal to another residence.'

Damned with faint praise by his Queen; spurned by the Prime Minister; dismissed by his employers, and deserted by his only friend—these were the final rewards for the man who had devoted his life to saving his fellow men from destruction.

Although he had spent so little time there, and had suffered so much at the hands of the people of Yarmouth, it was nevertheless a heart-breaking wrench to leave his home after forty years. He had talked of moving somewhere quite remote where his name would be honoured; but when it came to the point, he settled only a few miles away. He took the lease of a little villa in the village of Southtown, now part of the conurbation of Great Yarmouth. It was a very modest house, the sort a small tradesman or a bank clerk might occupy. There were two living rooms, three bedrooms and a kitchen in the basement. It stood on high ground, and from the window of the back bedroom he could look out across the river Yare to the Nelson Pillar, and beyond to the sea and the shipping anchored in the Roads.

It was a view he spent many hours contemplating; but most of the time he was seeing what was not there—beside the Nelson Pillar, another monument to Manby. He sketched the scene, and had it engraved as a letter heading for his notepaper, with the caption: 'View from Prospect Place, Southtown, Yarmouth. Especially the spot near the Nelson Pillar where the First Life was saved from Shipwreck by means of a rope attached to a shot fired from a Mortar, over the stranded vessel on the 12th of February, 1808.' His suggestion to the Mayor that this spot should be immortalised in stone, was met by a haughty refusal.

The idea of some indestructible memorial to his life's work became an obsession. He drew up a number of designs for monuments to himself; some were extremely elaborate; but he finally settled for a simple granite cube, with a grappling iron as the sole ornament. He induced a local stonemason to carry out his design on credit, and when it was finished, he had the monument set up on a pedestal in the minute front garden of his villa. It blocked the light of the sitting room window, and only just left room to reach the front door; but these were inconveniences Manby was happy to endure, and they did not concern his wife, who was now bedridden. The shock of the enforced move had brought on a stroke which had left her partially paralysed. Now that his monument was in position, Manby renamed the villa Pedestal House; it sounded well, and had a spacious ring to it which disguised the humble reality.

Sophia died on a Sunday in October 1843. Manby scarcely seemed to notice. His mind was now obsessed with a new project, an autobiography. It was his fixed determination, he said, to place before the public the motives that had induced the cruel and wanton attacks to blast his reputation and destroy his fame, and also the unprincipled conspiracy to throw him into poverty. On the day his wife died, he wrote to Dawson Turner, demanding the return of all the biographical material that was in his possession. When this letter was finished, an afterthought occurred to him.

He scrawled across the top of the page: 'Mrs Manby died this day.'[8]

Now that he was utterly alone, he decided to turn his little house into a Nelson Museum. He was the only man now in existence, as far as he had been able to prove, who had been a schoolfellow of the 'venerated Chief' seventy-six years ago. For years he had collected mementos of Nelson—engraved portraits, battle scenes, newspaper cuttings, a letter or two, and, most prized of all, a geranium which had been on board the *Victory* during the battle of Trafalgar. Not the actual plant, which Nelson had given to the North Sea Pilot, but one grown from a cutting.[9] He had so many exhibits, the front room was too small to display them properly. He called in a builder and told him to knock down the interior wall, 'thereby obtaining', he wrote proudly, 'a room of 22 feet in length, which I have termed my Nelson Gallery'.[10] Manby himself moved down into the basement. He made a study of a dark little room next to the kitchen. Here, with the aid of a simple, semi-literate amanuensis who came in every morning from the village, he worked on his autobiography, one ear hopefully alert for a ring on the front door bell, which would signal the arrival of an applicant to view the Nelson Gallery, or the visit of a friend.

The rings were few and far between. No one seemed any longer to be interested in Nelson, and certainly not in Manby's pathetic collection. As for social visits, no one dared befriend him, he said, for fear of offending the powerful Gooches. The loneliness, the sense of isolation, became unbearable. He decided to move. He would let the villa, and find a little place near London. He felt sure he could sell his Nelson collection for a substantial sum; but when he tried to do so, he found that no one wanted it at any price. In the end he gave it to the King's Lynn Museum; they did not want it either, but were obliged to accept.[11] Remnants of it still survive, hidden away in cupboards.

Manby did not move. He had become too old and weak to make the effort. The energy, the will-power and the enthusiasm which had kept him going seemed to drain away. He could no longer work consistently; more and more of his time he spent sitting at his bedroom window, staring out to sea where the ugly funnels of steamships were usurping the elegance of sail.

He died at his bedroom window, a tiny, shrivelled old man of eighty-nine. It had been hope that had kept him alive so long; often hope had faltered and grown very dim, but it had always rallied. There had always been another, brighter prospect just around the corner. But now there were no more corners, and no bright prospects. Only the bleak North Sea faced him, mocking his failure and sharing his solitude.

NOTES

Manby's correspondence with Dawson Turner has been drawn upon so extensively that where this source is clear from the context, no note has been appended.

Abbreviations used:
DT = Dawson Turner's Collected Papers, Wren Library, Trinity College, Cambridge
BM = British Museum Manuscript Collection
PRO = Public Records Office
NCA = Norfolk County Archives
GWM = George William Manby

CHAPTER ONE

Except where indicated by a separate note, this chapter is based on Manby's *Reminiscences*, the manuscript of which is in the British Museum (Add. MS. 29893). A modified version was printed, but never published.

1 Since this was written, the monument has been moved into the Maritime Museum, to protect it from the attention of vandals.

2 GWM's pamphlet *A Description of the Nelson Museum formed at Pedestal House*

3 DT
4 DT
5 Charles Philip Yorke represented Cambridge for twenty years, and became Secretary at War under Addington. His dubious claim to distinction is the campaign he waged to retain the practice of mutilating the bodies of executed traitors.
6 BM Add. MS. 35663/6. Cambridge Militia Records
7 These charges were brought at the so-called 'Delicate Investigation' of 1806. They were later revived at the trial of Queen Caroline.
8 The mysterious, and pathetic, William Austin.
9 *An Englishman's Reflections on the Author of the Present Disturbances*

CHAPTER TWO

1 *Reminiscences.* The Chevalier was a French secret agent, soldier and adventurer, whose sex was never definitely determined. At this time, having lost a pension through the Revolution, the Chevalier was eking out a living giving fencing demonstrations.
2 *Reminiscences*
3 *Fugitive Sketches of the History and Natural Beauties of Clifton. The History and Antiquities of the Parish of St. Davids, South Wales*
4 Dawson Turner (1775–1858) inherited a large fortune, and a bank, from his father. He left a collection of over 40,000 letters.
5 GWM's *Directions for Saving Persons from Vessels Stranded on a Lee Shore*
6 The invention of John Winn, a Yarmouth shipbuilder.
7 *Reminiscences*
8 There were other claimants, but Manby gave the credit to Burlton.
9 *Reminiscences*
10 ibid.
11 ibid.
12 John Bell (1747–1798), son of an eccentric hatter who ruined himself attempting to find longitude, served in the ranks before his ingenious gunnery inventions gained him a commission.
13 Society of Arts 'Transactions'. Vol. 10.
14 GWM's 'Essay on the Most Efficacious Means of Preserving the Lives of Shipwrecked Sailors'
15 House of Commons Proceedings. Session 1809. Vol. 10.
16 DT

CHAPTER THREE

1 PRO. 'Manby's Apparatus'
2 ibid.

3 The medals are now in the British Museum.

4 GWM's 'Essay on the Means of Saving Persons from Drowning when Falling through the Ice'

5 DT

6 'Address to the President of the Royal Society of Arts'

7 Sir Thomas Gooch was High Sheriff for Suffolk. He died, aged 81, in 1826.

8 GWM's 'Essay on the Extinction and Prevention of Destructive Fires'

CHAPTER FOUR

1 DT

2 GWM's *Journal of a Voyage to Greenland*

3 William Scoresby was the son of a prosperous whaling captain. Before following in his father's footsteps, he served as a seaman in the Navy. He was the author of many scientific works relating to the Arctic. Later in life he left the sea and entered the ministry.

4 William and John Cantiloe Joy. Examples of their work are in the Victoria and Albert Museum. William was about to be apprenticed to a plumber when Manby discovered him.

5 DT

6 DT

7 The *Baffin*, launched in 1820, cost £10,000 to build. She was specially designed for Arctic service, her bows being seven foot of solid oak.

8 *Journal of a Voyage to Greenland*

9 ibid.

10 DT

11 DT

12 DT

13 GWM's 'Plan for a Convict Colony in Greenland'

14 DT

15 In justice to Sir William Hillary, the R.N.L.I. undoubtedly owes its continued existence to his efforts. He spent a fortune building and equipping lifeboats, and died penniless as a result.

CHAPTER FIVE

This chapter is based almost entirely upon Manby's descriptive letters to Dawson Turner.

CHAPTER SIX

1 DT

2 DT

3 Manby may have been deterred by the possibility that he would be invited to take a hand at whist. Lord Granville was notorious for his deep play, and was known in Paris as 'the Wellington of Gamblers'. He once lost £20,000 at a sitting.

4 DT

5 DT

6 *Reminiscences*

7 DT

8 DT

9 DT

10 Sir Herbert Taylor had also been secretary to the Duke of York, who appointed him Adjutant-General.

11 DT

12 Sir Robert Waller Otway. At this time Otway was a Vice-Admiral, and had just returned from South America where he had been C-in-C. He was an Irishman, which may account for the element of blarney in his dealings with Manby.

CHAPTER SEVEN

1 DT. An over-optimistic suggestion by Lord Melbourne's secretary.

2 DT

3 PRO. Admiralty Experiments.

4 George Fowler Hastings was the son of the Earl of Huntingdon. He had a distinguished naval career, becoming Commander at the Nore.

5 DT

6 DT

7 DT

8 DT

9 DT. The only trial report which appears to have survived among the Admiralty papers in the Public Records Office is that of the two-shot device. Manby fired ten shells in ten minutes, all passing through the target, while a conventional gun, manned by picked naval gunners, fired only six shots in the same time. See also *A Short History of Early Life-Saving Apparatus*, by William H. Ffiske.

10 DT

11 They seem never to have been heard of again.

CHAPTER EIGHT

1 GWM's 'Plan for the Establishment of a Metropolitan Fire Police'

2 DT

3 Sir James Robert Graham (1792–1861). First Lord in Grey's administration. He was later to be Home Secretary under Peel, and was the centre of an uproar over the interception of M.P.s' letters.

4 DT. Manby sent Dawson Turner a verbatim account of both the toast and his reply.

CHAPTER NINE

1 There are now roughly 350 Coastguard Stations with the rocket equipment.

2 DT

3 DT

4 DT

5 DT

6 DT

7 James Silk Buckingham was a colourful character with a stormy and romantic past. He had gone to sea at the age of ten, and had been taken prisoner by the French while still in his teens. He was thrown out of India for criticising the government in his *Calcutta Journal*. As M.P. for Sheffield, he was a tireless champion of social reform, temperance and the abolition of flogging in the Navy.

CHAPTER TEN

1 Sir William Sidney Smith was another of the naval men accused with Thomas Manby of impropriety with Princess Caroline. When he retired, he married the widow of Sir George Berriman Rumbold and settled in Paris. He was the step-grandfather of Sir Cavendish.

2 DT

3 DT

4 Charles the Tenth abdicated on August 2nd, 1830, after Paris had taken up arms in protest against his restrictive regime.

CHAPTER ELEVEN

1 DT

2 DT

3 DT

4 Baron Glenelg was Colonial Secretary in Melbourne's second administration formed in April 1835.

5 DT. Manby sent Dawson Turner a full description of the incident.

6 DT

7 Augustus Frederick, Duke of Sussex, was the sixth son of George the

Third. He was President of the Royal Society, and Patron of the Royal Society for the Encouragement of Arts.

CHAPTER TWELVE

1 Discoverer of the Magnetic Pole.
2 DT
3 This was the origin of the present day Technical College, still in Regent Street.
4 DT
5 GWM's 'Address to the British Public, With Some Suggestions for the Recovering of Sunken Property' appeared dedicated to Her Majesty Victoria, Queen of the British Isles.
6 The model is now in the East Anglian Maritime Museum.

CHAPTER THIRTEEN

1 NCA. GWM to Robert Cole
2 ibid.
3 BM. Add. MS. 40506/7 and 40589. Correspondence of Sir Robert Peel
4 BM
5 BM
6 BM
7 NCA. GWM to Josiah French
8 DT
9 NCA. GWM to Robert Cole
10 DT
11 Correspondence in King's Lynn Museum

INDEX

Index

Medals, Manby's, 43, 66, 68, 79, 99, 120, 122, 126, 128, 130, 134–6, 153, 162 (note)
Melbourne, Lord, 97, 131, 133, 135, 140
Monument, Manby's, 11, 157, 160 (note)

Napoleon, 19, 23–5, 61
Navy, British, 16, 26, 30, 43, 94, 100, 133
Nelson, Admiral Lord, 12–13, 16–17, 28, 88, 158
— Gallery, 158, 160 (note)
— Pillar, 12–13, 156–7
Netherlands, King of, 120
Norfolk, 13, 20, 41, 43, 79, 109
Norris Castle, 89
Norwich Museum, 151

Ordnance, Board of, 33, 36
Orléans, Duke of, 65–6
Otway, Sir Robert Waller, 82–4, 86, 163 (note)

Palmerston, Lord, 129, 131
Peel, Sir Robert, 57, 79, 114, 131, 151, 153–5
Perceval, Spencer, 38
Pogson, Captain, 12, 18, 78
Police, Parliamentary Committee, 96–7
Polytechnic, Regent Street, 145–7, 149, 165 (note)
Portugal, Queen of, 87
Preston, Jane (first Mrs G. W. Manby), 21, 45
Prouting, John, 35

Reminiscences, Manby's, 160 (note)
Rockets, 108, 164 (note)
Ross, Captain John, 92, 143
Rowan, Colonel, 97, 104
Royal National Lifeboat Institution, 59

173